CW01559197

Jonathan Swift's
Gulliver's Travels

By the same author

Property and Landscape, George Philip, 1987

CRITICAL STUDIES OF
KEYTEXTS

Jonathan Swift's
Gulliver's Travels

Liz Bellamy

HARVESTER
WHEATSHEAF

New York   London   Toronto   Sydney   Tokyo   Singapore

First published 1992 by
Harvester Wheatsheaf
Campus 400, Maylands Avenue
Hemel Hempstead
Hertfordshire, HP2 7EZ
A division of
Simon & Schuster International Group

Typeset in 10½/12pt Sabon
by Keyboard Services, Luton, Beds

Printed and bound in Great Britain by
Biddles Ltd, Guildford and King's Lynn

British Library Cataloguing in Publication Data

A catalogue record for this book is available from
the British Library

ISBN 0 7450 0757 0 (hbk)
ISBN 0 7450 0758 9 (pbk)

---

1 2 3 4 5   96 95 94 93 92

Contents

Note on the Text

Gulliver's Travels was originally published in 1726, but there is some debate over the reliability of this text. It has been suggested that the manuscript was 'revised' by the publisher, Benjamin Motte. Swift's friend, Charles Ford, altered the text in several copies of Motte's first edition, and in 1735 the Dublin publisher, George Faulkner, used one of these copies as the basis for the *Gulliver's Travels* volume in his edition of Swift's *Works*. Opinions differ over whether this represents the restitution of Swift's original version, or revisions introduced with or without the consent of the author. All references to *Gulliver's Travels* included in this text have been taken from the Penguin edition (Harmondsworth, 1967; reprinted for Penguin Classics, 1985) edited by Peter Dixon and John Chalker, which represents a judicious blend of the Motte and Faulkner versions.

Preface

Gulliver's Travels is a biting satire which embodies the factionalism and the complex rhetoric of early eighteenth-century
politics; a traveller's tale that exploits and undermines the
enthusiasm for exploration of the reading public; a prose
narrative that manifests the uncertainty and flexibility of the
nascent novel form. Swift's ironic structure is essentially protean. It fulfils a range of functions, but it is also extremely
hard to pin down. The reader is expected to perform a very
active role, assessing and evaluating the multivalent text, to
construct an interpretation of the moral and political meaning,
while the irony continually upholds an image of how this
meaning might be misread by a spectral, omnipresent wrong
reader. The process of reading *Gulliver's Travels* does not,
therefore, provide the reassurance of the validation of established conventions and traditions, but continually subverts,
questions and destabilises. This textual strategy reinforces the
narrative questioning of the social and political structures, as
Swift attacks the commercial society and the system of colonial
oppression, dramatising the ambivalence towards Imperial
culture that he himself experienced as a member of the Anglo-
Irish elite. In this account of *Gulliver's Travels* I will analyse the
complex satirical structure to bring out the central ambivalence,
showing that within Swift's vision of political stability can be
discerned recurrent uncertainties – about national identity, the
primitive and the civilised, and ultimately about human nature
itself.

I

Contexts

Historical and Cultural Context

The historical and cultural context of the production of *Gulliver's Travels* was more than just a series of events, like the rise of the Whigs or the publication of Pope's 'Essay on Man'. It was a nexus of social, political and literary preoccupations which constituted a range of ways of seeing and describing the world, and a set of anxieties about how that world was organised, and whether such a complex system could ever be fully understood. *Gulliver's Travels* needs to be read in terms of these cultural concerns, but it is also evidence of them. It embodies the dynamism of the relationship between text and context, but it also highlights the dangers of seeking a univocal message from an equivocal text. The narrative structure manifests the diverse perspectives employed in the exploration of eighteenth-century society, but the text also displays the extent of the anxiety that motivated this exploration.

In the eighteenth-century political sphere much of this anxiety was focused around the parties or factions. Over recent years there has been considerable, and often very heated, historical debate over the function and importance of party in the eighteenth century. It has been argued that the two basic groupings, the Whigs and the Tories, were merely alliances of convenience, used by individuals to further their pursuit of personal power. Other historians have emphasised a different political division, between the 'court' interest of the administration, and the 'country' interest which stressed the traditional values of the gentry, and attacked the corruption it identified as almost synonymous with political power.[1]

It is certainly the case that the terms Whig and Tory cannot be used as in any way comparable to modern party labels. Individuals could and did change sides in the course of their careers, without the need for elaborate ideological justification. On the other hand, it would appear that although there was considerable debate and uncertainty in the eighteenth century over the definition of Whig and Tory, these terms were of considerable importance to the elite. Being a Whig or a Tory said something about not only your allegiance, but also your outlook on life. The labels had some meaning, even though, as we shall see in *Gulliver's Travels*, the distinctions were often subtle, and changed over time.

But there is a sense in which the *actual* role of party divisions was irrelevant to *Gulliver's Travels*. The political context of Swift's work was rhetorical and ideological, rather than psephological or parliamentary. What mattered was the way that politics was perceived, and the terms in which it was discussed and described, rather than how we might say it worked in practice. And it is in this realm of perception that the great anxiety over party was located. Swift and many of his contemporaries believed that since the Restoration of 1660, but more particularly since the death of Queen Anne in 1714, party had become increasingly important in the organisation of politics. But it was after 1720, when power and place were monopolised by Sir Robert Walpole and his Whig administration, that the attack on party became particularly heated. It was argued that the very existence of interest groups detracted from the pursuit of the public interest. As a result, party was identified with corruption.

This attack on party was itself a product of the political factionalism of the eighteenth century. It represented a basically Tory rhetoric which was increasingly used to undermine the Whig government. By identifying the administration as a faction tied together to share the spoils of office, and by condemning the whole idea of political divisions and groupings, the Tories sought to portray themselves not as a partial interest group, but rather as the embodiment of the public interest. Safe in the belief that they were neither a party nor a faction, but rather the defenders of Old England, the Tories were free to rail at will against the corruptions and divisions of the British political system.

This is not to say, however, that the deploring of faction was purely politic. Swift wrote at a time when the intellectual climate was dominated by the conflict between two opposing systems of rhetoric and values — between on the one hand what can be loosely described as the Tory, country interest, and on the other the Whig, court party. This conflict was far-reaching and largely genuine, but it was accompanied by an equally genuine sense of anxiety and regret that politics was so divided. *Gulliver's Travels* manifests the anxiety, but also the ideological combativeness, that characterised the age. Moreover Swift's personal political position typifies the complexity and fluidity of the party system of the period. He writes like a Tory, and his main period of political activity was in support of the Tories Harley and Bolingbroke – but he always described himself as an old Whig.[2] Swift believed that the Whigs had deserted their political principles, so that the Tories were the true Whigs of the day.

The preoccupation with party in the period from the Restoration to the mid-eighteenth century was connected with developments in a whole range of literary genres. In the poetry of John Dryden, Rochester and Alexander Pope, in the drama of John Gay, and in the periodical journalism of writers from Joseph Addison and Richard Steele to Delariviere Manley and Henry Fielding, the techniques of irony and satire were extensively exploited. The fact that large areas of literary production were based around the denigration of individuals or ideologies, and the explosion in the use of literary tropes like bathos, hyperbole and allegory, no doubt helped to fuel the belief that society and politics were becoming more and more factional. But it may also have been the case that the prevalence and resonance of faction encouraged the development of satiric literary forms.

Gulliver's Travels clearly needs to be seen in the context of this public, political significance of irony and satire, but it is also the product of a more particular and personal satiric vision, having been produced towards the end of a literary career that involved the utilisation of a whole range of ironic positions and voices to explore contemporary social and political realities. *A Tale of a Tub*, published in 1704, presents a central allegory of the condition of Christianity in the hands of Catholic, Anglican and dissenting Churches, but weaves around and through this symbolic narrative a series of digressions and distractions. These have the particular function of sending up contemporary pamphlets and works of criticism, but they also continually moderate, undermine and redefine the relationship between reader and both the text and the narrative voice. As John Traugott puts it:

> The demonic joy with which Swift conjures up his repertoire of voices in the *Tale* and speaks his deepest thoughts in their tongues, the sheer invention and flamboyant virtuosity, seem at times to define a game, civilized though Pyrrhonist and cynical, for would-be ironists, and we could accept it as such were it not for the deadly hatred and rage that show everywhere in odd, sudden bursts that it is not finally a game at all.[3]

The *Tale*'s narrator tells of three brothers (Anglicanism, Catholicism and dissent) who inherit a set of clothes (Christian theology), which they cut about in various ways to suit their own tastes and the fashions of the times. But in retailing this allegory, the narrator also unfolds his own tale, of his life as a hack writer. As the fantastic parodic structure develops, the construction of an essentially unreliable narrator provides an ironic reflection on the assumptions behind the presentation of narrative. At the same time it symbolises the underlying vision of a society rooted in uncertainty and confusion. The *Tale* is playful and comic, as John Traugott suggests, but it is a black comedy.

The parodic and protean style that was exploited in the *Tale*, and formed the basis for so many of Swift's subsequent works, drew on a tradition of satiric writing that went back to Thomas More and Erasmus.[4] This tradition made extensive use of allegory, irony and digression to ensure that the reader had a central role in the construction of the moral, social and philosophical narrative, but also to deny the reader the basic verities that make the reading process reassuring. We are forced into a position of questioning, by continually having our relationship to the narrative undermined. In the writing of François Rabelais there is a similar use of the flexible and often ironic narrative form, but while More and Erasmus represented a cerebral satiric tradition, Rabelais' method is frequently burlesque.[5] He has thus been hailed as an antecedent for those aspects of Swift's work which in the eighteenth century were termed 'low'. Moreover there are certain specific resemblances, in that Rabelais' eponymous heroes, Gargantua and Pantagruel, are giants, and the exploitation of the comic portrayal of differences in size anticipates some of the scenes of books one and two of the *Travels*.

Gulliver's Travels therefore needs to be set in the context of the politics of the period, and the tradition of philosophical satire, but there was also an immediate literary and social context. It has been customary to relate the work of Swift to an 'Augustan milieu', in the form of the writings of Alexander Pope and John Gay, with whom he joined, with John Arbuthnot, in the formation of the Scriblerus Club. Writing under the name of Martin Scriblerus, this group of writers produced a set of playfully satiric papers which anticipated elements of both the form and content of Lawrence Sterne's more famous *Tristram Shandy*. But while it is possible to detect various, often quite specific, Scriblerian references within *Gulliver's Travels*,[6] this emphasis on the Augustan context of Swift's writing needs to be moderated by a consciousness that Swift had a rather different perspective from his Scriblerian friends.

Carole Fabricant has indicated the extent to which Swift was a product of an Irish rather than an English landscape, and the peculiar circumstances of his native land coloured the terms of his presentation of society.[7] Ireland in the eighteenth century was endowed with an emasculated parliament, and was in practice under the political and economic dominance of England.

The Navigation Acts, passed between 1660 and 1663, dictated that all exports to the British colonies had to be made through English ports, while specific Acts put exorbitant duties on the sale of Irish cattle and wool to England. These Acts served as a considerable boost to the smuggling trade, but they also achieved their desired aim of stunting the economic development of Ireland. The mentor of Swift's early years, Sir William Temple, argued in his *Essay upon the Advancement of Trade in Ireland* (1673) that '[where] the Trade of *Ireland* comes to interfere with any main branches of the *Trade* of England . . . the encouragement of such Trade ought to . . . give way to the Interest of . . . Trade in England'.[8]

In his *Drapier's Letters* Swift attacked the 'grossest suppositions' that the English entertained of Ireland:

> As to *Ireland*, they know little more than they do of *Mexico*; further than that it is a country subject to the King of *England*, full of Boggs, inhabited by wild *Irish Papists*, who are kept in Awe by mercenary Troops sent from thence: And their general Opinion is, that it were better for *England* if this whole Island were sunk into the Sea.[9]

While Swift attempted to operate in the world of high English politics, he was inevitably influenced by his knowledge of the life of the inhabitants of England's subject neighbour.

But there is also a generic context to his work, for *Gulliver's Travels* was a prose narrative, and while it is often instructive to read it alongside the poetry of Pope and the drama of Gay, it needs to be seen in relation to the emergent fictional genre. At the time when Swift was writing, the conventions of fiction had yet to be fixed. There was no established genre of the novel, but instead there was a plethora of prose narratives, which took a range of forms and fulfilled a variety of social, moral and political functions. *Gulliver's Travels* is a political satire, embodying the rhetorical conflicts and factionalism of the early eighteenth century and drawing on an earlier tradition of satirical writing. But it can also be read as an example of a much more modern form of fictional writing, and a contribution to the debate over the nature of the novel.[10] For *Gulliver's*

Travels represents an exploration of the nature of the novel, and of the relationship between author, text and reader. Our understanding of the dynamics of Swift's text, and of the development of the role of the reader, conditions how we interpret the political allegory.

Critical Reception

Like most eighteenth-century novels, *Gulliver's Travels* was published anonymously. And as with most eighteenth-century novels, the identity of its author rapidly became an open secret. But for a while after its appearance, Swift pretended to disown the book, so that even in letters to his nearest and dearest friends, he refers to it as the work of a third person. This illusion was maintained by most of his correspondents, but they made sure that the anxious author – then in Ireland – was fully informed of how his book was being received in London. John Arbuthnot assured Swift that 'Gulliver is in everybody's hands',[1] and Alexander Pope prophesied that it would 'be hereafter the admiration of all men'.[2] John Gay described how:

> About 10 days ago a book was published here of the travels of one Gulliver, which hath been the conversation of the whole town ever since: the whole impression sold in a week; and nothing is more diverting than to hear the different opinions people give of it, though all agree in liking it extremely . . . From the highest to the lowest it is universally read, from the cabinet council to the nursery.[3]

Arbuthnot, Pope and Gay were friends of Swift, and were writing to Swift, and so we cannot take their testimony as gospel, but it is clear that *Gulliver* became an immediate fashionable success. It was reported that 10,000 copies were sold in the first week. This popularity owed something to the political allegory, which was lapped up by a public nourished on works of periodical journalism by writers such as Fielding,

Manley and Swift himself, which couched political comment and political scandal in metaphoric or symbolic terms. An indication of this can be discerned beneath Pope's assurances that:

> I find no considerable man very angry at the book. Some, indeed, think it rather too bold, and too general a satire; but none that I hear of accuse it of particular reflections – I mean no persons of consequence, or good judgement; the mob of critics, you know, always are desirous to apply satire to those they envy for being above them.[4]

Likewise Gay wrote that:

> The politicians to a man agree, that it is free from particular reflections, but that the satire on general societies of men is too severe. Not but we now and then meet with people of greater perspicuity, who are in search for particular applications in every leaf; and it is highly probable we shall have keys published to give light into Gulliver's design.[5]

According to Arbuthnot, Erasmus Lewis complained that the work required a key,[6] and a number of literary entrepreneurs satisfied the general interest by producing Gulliver keys of their own. Others found the satire so transparent that they could see no need for such aids to interpretation. One of the earliest and ablest of Swift's critics, Abel Boyer, wrote that the

> ALLUSIONS AND ALLEGORIES . . . are, for the most part so strong, so glaring and so obvious, that a Man must be a great Stranger to the World, in general, and to *Courtiers, Statesmen, Corrupt Senators, Rakes of Quality, Lawyers, Physicians, Virtuosi, Soldiers, Sharpers*, and *Women*, in particular, to have need of a KEY.[7]

As the words of Pope and Gay indicate, it was not quite the done thing amongst 'persons of consequence' to write particular rather than general satire. But while Swift's friends denied the existence of any specific references, it is clear that there were many others who were more than happy to search them out. That this was not entirely contrary to Swift's design is clear from his own reflection on the political allegory of *Gulliver's Travels* that:

11

Though the present age may understand well enough the little hints we give, the parallels we draw, and the characters we describe, yet this will all be lost the next. However, if these papers should happen to live till our grandchildren are men, I hope they may have curiosity enough to consult the annals and compare dates, in order to find out.[8]

Much of the initial discussion of *Gulliver's Travels* was taken up with this analysis of the extent of the individual references, and this theme has been reawakened in recent years, with the debate between, among others, the particularist John Downie and the generalist F. P. Lock.[9] But in the eighteenth century attention soon turned to the nature of the general philosophy. Samuel Johnson outlined the changing reactions to the book in the chapter on Swift in his *Lives of the English Poets*:

This important year [Johnson refers to 1727, although the *Travels* was actually published in 1726] sent likewise into the world *Gulliver's Travels*, a production so new and strange, that it filled the reader with a mingled emotion of merriment and amazement. It was received with such avidity, that the price of the first edition was raised before the second could be made; it was read by the high and the low, the learned and illiterate. Criticism was for a while lost in wonder; no rules of judgment were applied to a book written in open defiance of truth and regularity. But when distinctions came to be made, the part which gave the least pleasure was that which describes the Flying Island, and that which gave the most disgust must be the history of the Houyhnhnms.[10]

The disgust was manifested as early as 1726, in an anonymous pamphlet attacking Swift's moral character as well as his novel. For although the author was prepared to accept that there was 'a great deal of wit and more invention' in the first three books, the representation in the fourth voyage of beasts that were superior to human beings was seen as:

So monstrously absurd and unjust, that 'tis with the utmost pain a generous Mind must endure the Recital; a man grows sick at the shocking things inserted there; his Gorge rises; he is not able to conceal his Resentment; and closes the Book with Detestation and Disappointment.[11]

Likewise the critic James Beattie, while allowing Swift's satire 'to be perfectly just, as well as exquisitely severe', attacked the fourth voyage as 'an absurd and an abominable fiction'. As he explained in his essay 'On Fable and Romance' of 1783:

> It is abominable: because it abounds in filthy and indecent images; because the general tone of the satire is exaggerated into absolute falsehood, and because there must be something of an irreligious tendency in a work, which, like this, ascribes the perfection of reason, and of happiness, to a race of beings, who are said to be destitute of every religious idea.[12]

In the course of the eighteenth century this became the standard criticism of *Gulliver's Travels*. The portrayal of the Houyhnhnms was regarded as an insult to humanity, and since Gulliver's opinions were identified with the views of his creator, Swift was increasingly represented as a moody misanthrope, driven to write by his hatred of the moral and physical character of mankind. This was the standard image of Swift in the prurient Victorian period, and it produced a kind of proto-psychoanalytical criticism, in which the role of the critic was not so much to disentangle the text, as to speculate over what might have driven the author to such a position. Particular attention was paid to the scatalogical element of his writing, with many critics sharing T. B. Macaulay's belief that Swift's mind was 'richly stored with images from the dung-hill and the lazar-house'.[13] The sparse details of Swift's personal life were rifled, and supplemented with copious conjecture, in order to endorse a reading of the novel as the product of a bitter and twisted mind. One of the most eloquent exponents of this approach was William Thackeray. His essay on 'The English Humourists of the Eighteenth Century' represents Swift almost as a psychological case study:

> As is the case with madmen, certain subjects provoke him, and awaken his fits of wrath. Marriage is one of these; in a hundred passages in his writings he rages against it; rages against children . . . What had this man done? What secret remorse was rankling at his heart? What fever was boiling in him that he should see all the world bloodshot?[14]

The distaste at books three and four persisted into this century, so that many took Leslie Stephen's advice that 'readers who wish to indulge in a harmless play of fancy will do well to omit the last two voyages; for the strain of misanthropy which breathes in them is simply oppressive.'[15] Moreover the traditional interpretation of the philosophical significance of the Houyhnhnms was widely held into the 1950s. Critics as diverse as Lucius Elder, Charles Forth, William Eddy, F. R. Leavis, Basil Willey and Arthur Case maintained the belief that book four embodied the eighteenth-century celebration of reason in its portrayal of admirable passionless Houyhnhnms and hateful irrational Yahoos. At the same time, there was a movement away from the nineteenth-century preoccupation with Swift the man, with the development of an industry of Swift scholarship which sought to trace the meaning and sources of his satire. In the 1920s and 30s this largely took the form of research into the real and imaginary voyages on which Swift's work was seen to be based, the most notable of such studies being William Eddy's *Gulliver's Travels: A critical study* of 1923, and Harold Williams' *Dean Swift's Library* of 1932. In 1937 Marjorie Nicolson and Nora Mohler revolutionised the interpretation of book three by demonstrating that the satire on scientific experiments was drawn not from Swift's active imagination, but from real experiments carried out by real scientists at the beginning of the eighteenth century.[16]

In the 1950s the focus of interest moved from the identification of sources to the translation of Swift's imaginary languages, with the publication of philological articles by Harold Kelling, Paul Clark and Roland Smith. In 1945 Arthur Case elucidated the political allegory, suggesting in his *Four Essays on 'Gulliver's Travels'* that not only books one and two, but also three and four, should be seen as having a primarily political function, revising the reading of Sir Charles Firth's article of 1919, 'The Political Significance of *Gulliver's Travels*'. In 'The Political Theory of *Gulliver's Travels*', Z. S. Fink emphasised Swift's support for a constitution derived from classical models, while F. P. Lock's *The Politics of Gulliver's*

Travels argued against the conventional allegorical reading, suggesting that the novel was based on general rather than particular satire. A rather different tradition of criticism was embodied in George Orwell's essay 'Politics vs. Literature: An examination of *Gulliver's Travels*', in which he condemned Swift's novel for the conservatism of its politics.[17]

The twentieth century has therefore seen the emergence of a new realm of Swift scholarship, and a new attitude to Swift's works. Critics no longer feel it necessary to apologise for dealing with such a smutty or distasteful subject, and have come, especially in the last thirty years, to emphasise the wit and humour rather than just the bleakness of the satire. Yet despite the use of new language and new techniques, some of the analyses can be seen as continuations or reorientations of various earlier critical traditions. The Freudian readings that emerged in the mid-twentieth century, in particular, can be seen as a perpetuation of the misanthropic readings of the nineteenth century. Evelyn Hardy's *The Conjured Spirit* of 1949, and Phyllis Greenacre's *Swift and Carroll: A psychoanalytic study of two lives* of 1955 emphasise the scatological aspects of Swift's work, and, like the earlier critics, tend to treat the writings as a source of evidence about the man.

This approach has been challenged by Norman O. Brown in his influential essay 'The Excremental Vision' of 1962. Brown does not seek to analyse Swift's scatology to find evidence of personal neurosis, but instead attempts 'to appreciate his insight into the universal neurosis of mankind'.[18] He suggests that the 'real' theme of poems such as *The Lady's Dressing Room*, with its famous line 'Celia, Celia, Celia shits' (though the crucial word is omitted from Brown's essay), 'is the conflict between our animal body, appropriately epitomized in the anal function, and our pretentious sublimations, more specifically the pretensions of sublimated or romantic platonic love'.[19] Whether or not you accept the detail of Brown's Freudian argument that Swift foreshadowed the psychoanalytic theory of sublimation as the key to human neurosis,[20] it is clear that Swift's 'excremental vision' was as much an exploration of the anality of the species, as a manifestation of any fetishes of his own.

In John Traugott's essay, 'The Yahoo in the Doll's House: *Gulliver's Travels* the children's classic', the sexual and scatalogical elements of Swift's satire are identified as part of a repertoire of techniques utilising play and childhood games. Traugott invokes Jean Piaget's psychological theory that doll play enables the child to act out the power relationships of her or his own life, and adopt the position of authority. But in Lilliput, Traugott suggests, 'this charming play metamorphoses into the bitter charades of political power'.[21] Swift presents a series of childish games which are also matters of real or political life or death, and in doing so exposes the perverse or arbitrary character of politics.

Perhaps the most notable growth area in Swift scholarship over the past thirty years has been the study of the philosophical allegory of book four, with critics divided between the 'soft' and the 'hard' interpretation of Houyhnhnm society. The 'soft' view was first laid out in the late 1950s by Kathleen Williams, Ernest Tuveson and Samuel Monk. It is based on the argument that Swift, as a Christian and defender of the established church, could not have wanted the atheistic Houyhnhnm society to be seen as an ideal. Instead it must be intended as a warning against an excessive reliance on reason. This reading helps to get round two problems previously encountered in the interpretation of book four: first, the fact that very few readers have ever found Houyhnhnm society at all attractive – 'the Houyhnhnms are dreary beasts' as George Orwell put it;[22] secondly, the fact that by the end of the book Gulliver appears to be completely mad, and cannot, therefore, be a very reliable guide and narrator. Yet many aspects of Swift's presentation of Houyhnhnm society suggest that it is supposed to be admirable, and these aspects are emphasised by the upholders of the 'hard' reading. This draws on Swift's adherence elsewhere in his works to a rationalist ethic, and argues that we should accept Gulliver's interpretation, and see Houyhnhnmland as a utopia which puts to shame the irrational society of erring, passionate humankind.

The development of the 'soft' reading to challenge the traditional 'hard' interpretation in many ways symbolised the change in the terms of the analysis of Swift's work that took place in the mid-twentieth century. Writers moved away from the unsympathetic view of Swift as a curious individual or an embodiment of the now alien ideology of his age. To support the reappraisal of both the man and his work, they emphasised the subtlety of his narrative structure, exposing the multiple levels of the irony, as well as the witticisms of the 'jocose dean'. This change is perhaps most clearly embodied in the criticism of Ricardo Quintana. Quintana has shifted from the almost nineteenth-century perspective of his *The Mind and Art of Jonathan Swift* of 1936, through an analysis of the rhetorical method of *The Tale of a Tub* in 1948, to the soft reading of the satire, and the sympathetic image of Swift that characterised his *Swift: An introduction* of 1955.

The critical conflict over book four has not really been re-solved, for in the 1960s and 70s a number of critics (Sherburn, Crane, Rosenheim, Landa, Greene, Rawson) resurrected and renovated the hard reading that had been orthodoxy in the 1930s and 40s, and fitted it out to join battle with the in-creasingly dominant soft approach. Some accounts of the novel have avoided opening the can of soft and hard worms altogether, either by limiting their handling of the issue to blithe references to Houyhnhnmland as both utopian and distopian, or by concentrating on other aspects of the book. Some of the most perceptive and fascinating of the readings of the past few decades have been those which have analysed particular facets of Swift's writings, ambience or ideology, in order to provide a new perspective on his works. A seminal work of this kind was Oliver Ferguson's *Swift and Ireland* of 1962, which examines Swift's ambivalent attitude to his native land. W. B. Carnochan's *Lemuel Gulliver's Mirror for Man* (1968) considers *Gulliver's Travels* in relation to seventeenth- and eighteenth-century theories of satire, and, more recently, Bertrand Goldgar, J. A. Downie and F. P. Lock have all looked at Swift's political allegiances in relation to the political rhetoric of the early eighteenth century. But perhaps the most original reading of recent years is Carole Fabricant's *Swift's Landscape*, which explores the turmoil and disorder of Swift's real and imaginary landscapes in order to emphasise the subversive elements in the work, and the disparity between the chaotic world vision of Swift and the stability that is taken to epitomise the Augustan ideal.

Theoretical Perspectives

Despite the range of approaches that has been used in the interpretation of *Gulliver's Travels*, its satirical form has ensured that even the most theoretically divergent analyses have tended to share a certain amount of common ground. In the writings of the twentieth century the terms of the discussion of the novel have generally been based around an essentially historicist core. The Freudians, the critics of Swift's personal character, even those advocates of the hard and soft readings who are preoccupied with the supposedly less political book four, have all to some extent located their analyses within a historical context, for the simple reason that this is the only way of making sense of many of Swift's allusions.

Perhaps the most notable attempt to make an exception to this rule is Brean Hammond's volume on *Gulliver's Travels* in the Open University's 'Open Guides to Literature' series. Hammond provides a detailed reading of the text in order to examine the distance between Gulliver and the 'implied narrator' – i.e. the extent to which Swift seems to want us to believe what Gulliver says. The terms of this discussion owe much to the reception theory outlined by Wolfgang Iser in *The Act of Reading*.[1] Iser demonstrates how narrative constructs an image of the ideal reader. The real readers have to relate their own readings to the reactions attributed to this implied ideal, while at the same time distinguishing between the author and the narrative voice. The use of this model of narrative in the Open Guide means that Hammond can provide a clear analysis of the experience of reading *Gulliver's Travels*, and can highlight the crucial issue of the role of Gulliver within the novel. Yet by concentrating on the words on the page, and by using extraneous historical material primarily as a means of elucidating particular readings, he necessarily restricts the range of interpretations that can be presented. Some understanding of Swift's cultural and political ambience is essential for an appreciation of the extent, implications and flexibility of his satire, and thus for a recognition of the multiple meanings of his work.

Swift's ideology is best understood not as a general reflection on the human condition, but as part of the cut and thrust of debate in an intensely partisan period. Likewise his utilisation of narrative conventions was not a purely personal achievement, an abstract manipulation of form. It needs to be seen in the context of the generic uncertainty that characterised the fiction of the early eighteenth century. Yet to say this is not to give a green light to all forms of turgidly historicist criticism. Over-reliance on the contextualisation of the novel can be just as dangerous as divorcing it from its cultural environment. Analysis may shade into antiquarianism, as each sentence of a work is glossed by historical explanation, filling in the details of the events and people that are being satirised. Of course we need to know what Swift's allegories are about, but the exposition should aid and not occlude our understanding of the dynamics of the text. *Gulliver's Travels* is more than simply a coded image of the events of the early eighteenth century, so that the cracking of the code should be a means of exposing its formal and ideological structures, rather than being an end in itself.

As a result, *Gulliver's Travels* demands analysis in terms which bring together some of the theoretical insights developed since the 1960s, with more traditional methods of interpretation. Many of the ideas articulated within works of critical thought have percolated down to the level of critical practice, and have drastically modified the ways in which narrative is seen to function. The French critics, Roland Barthes and Michel Foucault, have suggested that the concept of the author as the creator of meaning, and the figure with ultimate authority over the text, is itself a historical construct, the product of a particular kind of society. In Barthes' 'The Death of the Author' and Foucault's 'What is an Author?' these writers have drawn an image of primitive society in which narrative is seen as the embodiment of collective consciousness. The celebration of the author as sole originator of the text is therefore not an inevitable consequence of literary creation, but rather is represented as the product of the development of capitalist ideology:

> The *author* is a modern character, no doubt produced by our society as it emerged from the Middle Ages, inflected by English empiricism, French rationalism, and the personal faith of the Reformation, thereby discovering the prestige of the individual, or, as we say more nobly, of the 'human person'.[2]

Barthes and Foucault have rejected the critical tradition that has emphasised the theological status of the author. They deny that the purpose of literary analysis is to ascertain 'what the author really meant', and instead have stressed the role of the reader in the construction of the work. Each reader creates her or his own text in the process of reading. Ideally, this process should not be one of closure – the shutting off of meanings – but should be a way of opening up the work's polysemous structure:

> The task of criticism is not to bring out the work's relationships with the author, nor to reconstruct through the text a thought or experience, but rather, to analyze the work through its structure, its architecture, its intrinsic form, and the play of its internal relationships.[3]

For Foucault, one of the major determinants of form is the kind of writing – the discourse – to which the work belongs. In *The Archaeology of Knowledge* he identifies the eighteenth century as a period which saw the emergence of numerous discrete 'languages' or ways of describing the world, such as the language of economics, and the language of botany.[4] For Barthes, reading is conditioned not so much by particular structures of meaning, as by the totality of meaning – it is an endless process of proliferation that draws on all the articulations – the writing, the discourse, the speech – that exist in the world.

Both these approaches owe much to the work of the Russian formalist critics of the 1920s and 30s, writers like Victor Shklovsky and Roman Jakobson.[5] These writers had identified the purpose of literature not as the communication of messages through naturalistic representation, but rather as the defamiliarisation of perception in order to stimulate a questioning of conventional assumptions. The formalists emphasised the importance of literary form, and instead of seeing literary change in the context of social change, they saw it rather as an autonomous, self-perpetuating series of styles. The formalist writers, therefore, like structuralist critics such as Barthes, and post-structuralist critics such as Foucault, have an essentially ahistorical approach to literature. They see developments in the various genres or discourses as having an internal dynamic, which is unaffected by any kind of exterior 'reality'. As may be clear from the fact that I have chosen to analyse a text like *Gulliver's Travels*, and as I have already indicated in discussing the context of that work, I cannot go as far as formalist or structuralist critics, in divorcing literature from the society which produced and consumes it.

Likewise I cannot accept the concept of the total autonomy of discourse. The political, economic and scientific debates of the eighteenth century were conducted within their own discursive conventions, and care is needed in distinguishing their different terms, but this does not mean that they should be considered as wholly separate, and irrelevant to a work of fiction like *Gulliver's Travels*. The narrator of the *Travels* takes up and satirises the terms of the various types of writing, and in doing so provides an indication of at once the importance and the superability of discursive barriers. *Gulliver's Travels* must be interpreted as a work of fiction, using the conventions of fictional analysis, but in conducting this analysis the critic must be aware of how the novelist can exploit, mimic, incorporate within the fictive structure, and thereby contribute to, debates within other areas of human endeavour.

The critical theory of Barthes and his followers has had its most direct impact on critical practice in the interpretation of writers like Bertold Brecht, Marcel Proust and Georges Bataille, who are exploring similar questions of language and narrative voice to those explored within the works of theory. But Barthes has also shown (most notably in *S/Z*, his analysis of Balzac's *Sarrasine*) how his techniques can be used to expose the multiplicity of meanings within texts conventionally interpreted through a search for a single 'right reading'.[6] But on the whole the critical theorists have not tended to pay a great deal of attention to the eighteenth century. With the exception of Lawrence Sterne's *Tristram Shandy*, which was identified by Victor Shklovsky as 'the most typical novel in world literature',[7] the eighteenth-century novel has frequently been ignored completely, or referred to in vague terms as if it were the lineal antecedent of the nineteenth-century novel. Yet the narrative techniques of the eighteenth century were very different from those employed in the Victorian period. Far from having the authoritative and wholly omniscient narrator that structuralist critics have sought to undermine, the eighteenth-century novel is frequently told by a character whose authority is highly dubious. Defoe's Moll Flanders, Captain Singleton and Colonel Jack are self-confessed thieves and liars, and even Fielding's apparently trustworthy narrators exploit the supposedly subordinate role of the reader, by repeated references to the unreliability of their own information or memory. In this way the novels of the eighteenth century explore those questions of the relationship of the text and the reader, and of the authority of the narrative voice, that were later to be explored in critical theory.

Tristram Shandy, with its preoccupation with the nature of narrative, was therefore the rule rather than the exception. But this is not to say that the eighteenth-century novel was in some way like the novels of the twentieth century – the work of James Joyce, Dorothy Richardson or Virginia Woolf. The writers and critics of the twentieth century were reacting against the formal conventions of realism of the standard

Victorian novel. The eighteenth-century novelists were writing before these conventions had been established. The early novels need to be seen in the context of contemporary ideas of the role and form of literature, but the emphasis on this kind of criticism is itself in part a product of the developments in literary theory of recent years. For while the architects of structuralism and post-structuralism can be accused of not having taken full account of the subtlety of the early fictional structures, the general recognition of that subtlety within critical practice was to a large extent dependent on the insights, and the general model of literary production, formulated by theorists. The theoretical perspective has initiated new methods of evaluation and analysis which can then be used to attack the historical trajectory behind the theory.

A number of critics have applied recent critical theory to *Gulliver's Travels*. Alain Bony's post-Saussurean account has analysed how the text constructs an illusory authorial presence, suggesting that Gulliver is only a product of the needs of the reader. The post-structuralist readings of Terry Castle and Grant Holly have considered the role of the text and of textuality within the novel, drawing attention to the extent to which Swift is himself preoccupied with the question of the uncertainty of meaning, and Terry Eagleton's Lacanian interpretation sees *Gulliver's Travels* as a reaction against 'that new obsessionally subject-centred literary *genre* which, much to Swift's ideological disgust, was in process of arising'. The chronology of Eagleton's reading is, however, rather confusing, for the emergence of the subject-centred literature is identified with the publication of Samuel Richardson's *Pamela* in 1740–1, while Swift was reacting in 1726.

Apart from these four short articles, there has been no heavily theoretical account of *Gulliver's Travels*. None the less, the developments in critical theory have had a considerable indirect impact on the terms of the analysis of the work, although in many ways they have tended to confirm the movement of criticism in directions initiated in the work of the 1940s and 50s. The questioning of the identity and authority of the narrative voice has encouraged the rejection of the misanthropic reading that gained general currency in the nineteenth century, but also of the hagiographic criticism that frequently replaced it. Gulliver is no longer assumed to be synonymous with Swift, and criticism has focused on the distance between the narrator's interpretation of events, and the interpretation constructed by the reader. This has exposed the range and flexibility of Swift's satiric structure, modified the reading of his political allegory and fuelled the debate between the advocates of the hard and the soft views of book four. In the ensuing reading of the text the critical approaches of dilute theory will be incorporated into a method that recognises the interaction of the text with its context. The result is a 'new historicist' form of criticism which is peculiarly appropriate for the interpretation of works such as *Gulliver's Travels*.

II

Gulliver's Travels: A Reading of the Text

1

Fact/Fiction: Some Ambiguities

In the early eighteenth century there was a tremendous craze in Britain for books of travel and exploration. The previous century had seen enormous improvements in navigational techniques and geographical knowledge, and as the proto-Imperialistic traders began to explore the exploitation of the earth's extremities, the public back home were eager for stories of wonders and adventures on the other side of the world. A considerable publishing industry developed to satisfy the voracious demand, and many ex-mariners and explorers were able to make a living recounting their observations and escapades. The resultant works ranged from basically scientific tracts and treatises, like those incorporated into the *Philosophical Transactions of the Royal Society*, to more exciting pieces in which observations on geography and natural history were juxtaposed with tales of piracy and mutiny on the high seas.[1]

One of the most famous and popular writers of the period was William Dampier (1652–1715) who, as ship's captain and sometime buccaneer, had travelled extensively across the globe. His *A New Voyage Round the World* was published in 1697, and contains a wealth of detailed information on the plants, animals and customs of the places he visited, as well as details of the manner and incidents of his life on board ship.[2] It is clear that Swift was intimately acquainted with the travel-writing genre: Gulliver refers to his 'cousin Dampier' (*GT* 37), and Swift records that in the Summer of 1722, while staying at Loughall, he read 'through abundance of Trash' including 'I know not how many diverting Books of History and Travels'.[3]

But by no means all the voyages published in the early eighteenth century were the product of the labours of genuine voyagers. In addition to the works of explorers like Dampier, William Cowley, Bartholomew Sharp and John Cox, there were innumerable works by armchair travellers. These combined descriptions of foreign parts plagiarised from authentic accounts, with passages that were simply made up. As Milton Voight explained, 'fraudulent travel accounts . . . were welcomed by the eighteenth-century public, which . . . was "travel-crazy".'[4]

One of the most famous travel writers of the early eighteenth century was a man who went by the name of George Psalmanazar. He pretended to be a native of the island of Formosa, and was author of *An Historical and Geographical Description of Formosa* of 1704. Psalmanazar was for a time lionised by London society and in particular was taken up by the Bishop of London. He explained away his fair complexion on the grounds that the ruling classes of Formosa did not have dark skins since they spent most of their lives underground, and having declared that Formosans never cooked their food, forced himself to eat all his meat raw whenever he was in public. Despite its fantastic extravagance and manifest improbability, his book was for a while widely accepted as a bona fide work of history and geography. In his will, Psalmanazar confessed what had, by the time of his death, been generally recognised – that *Formosa* 'was no other than a meer forgery . . . a scandalous imposition on the public, and such as I think myself bound to beg God and the world pardon for writing'.[5]

Psalmanazar's work was, however, only an extreme example of a general tendency towards the fictitious and fantastic that ran through travel writing in the late seventeenth and early eighteenth centuries. Even genuine voyagers frequently spiced up their works through the exercise of the imagination, and between the wholly prosaic and scientific, and the wholly spurious, there was an extensive grey area of works that combined elements of fact and fiction. *Gulliver's Travels* both satirised and exploited the existence of this grey area. If *Gulliver's Travels* had been the product of a society like ours, predicated on a general belief in the total dissociation of the realms of science and imagination, the meaning and purpose of the book would have been quite clearly and unequivocally allegorical. As it was, Swift was writing for an audience who did not always find it necessary to discriminate between truth and falsity, or, at least, were prepared to enjoy supposedly scientific works that stretched the bounds of credibility. As a result, *Gulliver's Travels* was not just a continuation of the tradition of political or philosophical allegory embodied in works such as Thomas More's *Utopia* or Francis Bacon's *New Atlantis*.[6] It also worked as both a contribution to, and satire on, the hugely popular travel-writing genre. Gulliver's tale mimics the style of contemporary voyages, with their incorporation of nautical jargon, and their attention to trivial domestic detail, and it mocks the improbability of the wilder works, by casting thoroughly fantastic adventures in the guise of truth. This does not negate the political or philosophical significance of the book, but it did mean that at the time of its creation, the allegory did not have to be the main structural imperative. Swift could move in and out of the allegory, because the book was basically held together by the voyage or pseudo-voyage format.

The location of Swift's political satire within a genre that was all too often characterised by falsity and exaggeration also coloured the presentation of contemporary society. There is a sense in which the traveller's tall tale can be seen as an appropriate medium for the portrayal of a social and moral fabric that is revealed as increasingly fantastic, but is also shown to be divorced from the solid principles of truth and common sense. Moreover the presentation of imaginary voyages in the form of a factual account served to satirise and undermine the supposedly authoritative narrative voice. Gulliver is the forthright sailor, incapable of saying 'the thing that is not' (*GT* 281), but he is also a stereotype of the hack writer, propagator of primitive and improbable fictions. By identifying his narrator as subject as well as mouthpiece for the satire, Swift emphasised the absence of any normative controlling perception within the work.

Swift's abdication of responsibility for the work is indicated at the very start of *Gulliver's Travels*, in the letter from the publisher to the reader. Richard Sympson presents himself as a relative of Gulliver's, who has abridged and edited the manuscript for publication. Swift's voice is thus concealed behind not one but two fictitious characters, and the details of the history of the text are expanded in the letter from Gulliver to Sympson appended to the 1735 Faulkner edition of the *Travels*. The construction of this kind of fiction about the origins of the manuscript was absolutely typical of the eighteenth-century novel.[7] The history of Defoe's Moll Flanders was represented as having been put, by an anonymous editor, into 'modester words than she told it at first', and the prefaces to innumerable works recount the circumstances in which the manuscript was found by the editor. It may have been used to wrap candles in a chandler's shop, or as gun wadding, or left in the room of a defaulting tenant, or amongst the papers of a deceased clergyman. Indeed, in Henry MacKenzie's *The Man of Feeling* the subterfuge is carried so far that numerous passages are missing from the book to represent the manuscript pages torn out by the clergyman who was using them as gun wadding.[8]

The construction of these elaborate fictions concerning the origins of the texts demonstrates the extent of the disparity between the novels of the eighteenth century, and the novels of the omniscient, authoritative narrators of the nineteenth century. While the readers of the Victorian novel tend to be guided through events by a narrative voice that shows them how they are expected to react and interpret, the readers of the eighteenth-century novel are often left in the hands of a figure who is either shadowy and mysterious, or characterised as unreliable.

Gulliver's Travels not only contains no voice that can be identified with Swift's, but goes out of its way to avoid any such identification by presenting the text through fictitious mediators, exploiting a form that is satirised as highly misleading. The reader finds that, like Gulliver himself, s/he is all at sea, in a world in which perspective is all important, but there is no single point of view from which to interpret events. Things are big or little depending on how you look at them, and Swift's text reveals that we can never be sure that we are looking the right way.

This radical decentring of the reader's role ensured the construction of a social and political vision that was peculiarly suited to Swift's philosophy and perspective. For Swift did not write from the centre of English culture and society, but from the margins. He was born into the Anglo-Irish elite, of English parents who had only recently settled in Ireland, and he seems to have been subject to the full force of the sense of dispossession and uncertainty that characterised this group.

The Anglo-Irish were neither Irish nor English. They were looked down on in England, as the products of a primitive, impoverished and barbarous landscape, but were often equally despised by the majority Catholic population of their native land, who saw them as alien oppressors, living off the labour of an exploited peasantry. The realities of Anglo-Irish rule were fully brought home to Swift in his role as incumbent of the parish of Kilroot near Belfast. Since the great majority of the population was either Catholic or Presbyterian, Swift ministered to only a handful of parishioners. Yet his was not a life of luxurious idleness. There is no evidence that the living of Kilroot provided him with a church to preach in, a manse to live in, or a glebe to cultivate.[9] Swift was acutely aware of the cultural differences that separated him from the majority Catholic population, but this sense of alienation was not accompanied by the material comforts that conventionally help to assuage the lot of the colonial oppressor. Swift's standard of living was far superior to that of the majority of his Catholic neighbours, but he felt it to be far inferior to that of his English colleagues.

Swift always said that he felt like an Englishman in Ireland

and an Irishman in England, and he was torn between a desire to be successful and respected in English society, manifested in his attempts to function as a major player on the English political stage, and a deeply rooted sympathy for, and sense of connection with, the native Irish population, manifested in Irish writings such as *The Drapier's Letters*. There was therefore a fundamental ambivalence running through Swift's attitudes to both Ireland and England. A sense of empathy for the problems of the Irish people was juxtaposed with a recurrent Anglo anxiety, which perceived Ireland as primitive, dangerous, unrestrained and unstable, and this uncertainty informed Swift's presentation of the Houyhnhnms and Yahoos in book four of *Gulliver's Travels*.

There was a long-established literary tradition of representations of Ireland as the mistress of England, as Dark Rosaleen and Kathleen ni Houlihan, and this idea was picked up by Swift in his allegorical narrative *The Story of the Injured Lady* (written 1707, published 1746). This portrays Ireland as a mistress, jilted by her lover (England) after his engagement to another (Scotland). The immediate stimulus for this was the planned Act of Union between Scotland and England of 1707, but it also provides a more generally applicable model of the relationship between England and Ireland. The concept of Ireland as a wronged woman, a gullible child in relation to the more sophisticated England, is combined with the suggestion that the figurative woman also has a sexuality of her own. Like her predecessors Dark Rosaleen and Kathleen ni Houlihan, she has a dark and mysterious sense of self that is beyond the understanding of the more civilised and sophisticated male. She is vulnerable, but she is aware of her rights, her desires and her integrity.

It has been a convention of colonial writing to represent the colonised country as female, subject to a dominant partner, and in basing his personal life around relationships with young, impressionable and seemingly 'subject' women, Swift appears to be replicating, at a private level, the model of imperial conquest. Yet the recurrence within Swift's writings of apparently misogynistic representations of the female body indicates a fundamental uncertainty over the stability or validity of this power relationship. There seems to be a lurking fear that within the tractable little girl lies the seeds of the fully sexualised woman, just as within the subject Irish nation may lie either primitive natural man or full-blown political rebellion. Hence Swift's ambivalent attitude towards the human form, and the female body in particular, and hence his 'excremental vision' - his potent and painful awareness that despite an appearance of cultivation, the individual is essentially physical. Whatever our pretensions, the inescapability of our biological functions constantly reinforces our basic corporeal nature, while providing a characteristically Swiftian satiric deflation of our intellectual pretensions.

Swift is torn by the conflict between concepts of civilisation and barbarism, between the refined and the natural, between the coloniser and the colonial oppressed. As Norman Brown has suggested in relation to the excremental vision, the fact that Swift's work manifests these ambivalences should not be seen as evidence of some kind of personal inadequacy or madness.[10] Swift is revealing the ambivalences and conflicts within society, but while Brown emphasises their psychological significance, I shall prioritise their social and political implications. Swift's concept of human nature was crucially tied to his anxiety over the relationship between Ireland and England, but also to wider issues of the nature of colonialism and imperialism, and a concern over the apparent fragmentation of society. These anxieties can be seen to be embedded in the structure of *Gulliver's Travels*, and the terms of its portrayal of political systems.

2

Looking Down: Lilliput

At the start of the voyage to Lilliput, Gulliver introduces himself not as the satiric butt and gullible clown that he is later to become, but rather as a figure on whose perceptions we ought to be able to rely. He is a younger son of a gentry family at a time when membership of the landed class was generally recognised as essential for an understanding of the structure of society.[1] He has been educated at Cambridge and Leyden, studied medicine, navigation, and mathematics, travelled in the East and West Indies, studying the manners and languages of the peoples and has read widely in both ancient and modern authors.[2] Such a background should make him ideally qualified to be an informed and trustworthy guide and narrator – even though some critics have suggested that his credibility is undermined by his apprenticeship to 'good master Bates' (*GT* 53).[3]

As a result, once Gulliver lands up on the island of Lilliput, the reader is inclined to accept his interpretation of events. That is, when Gulliver is lying on the ground surrounded by people 6 inches high, we assume, not that such a thing ever actually happened, but that the view of events we are expected to adopt is essentially based on the perspective of Gulliver. The text invites us to look down on the Lilliputians, rather than up at the narrator, and the view we are given is at first largely favourable. The Lilliputians are hospitable, brave, efficient and prudent; they are 'most excellent mathematicians, and arrived to a great perfection in mechanics' (*GT* 61).

Gulliver's initial praise of the Lilliputians reflects on the situation pertaining in Britain in the early eighteenth century. The character of the Emperor, with his striking and masculine appearance, his graceful and majestic deportment, his plain apparel and clear voice (*GT* 65), inevitably highlighted the limitations of the British monarch, George I, who was notorious for his corpulence, excessive ugliness, profligate extravagance and guttural accent. The Emperor of Lilliput lives primarily off the income from his own lands, only raising taxes from his subjects in exceptional circumstances, and the defence of his realm is ensured not just by professional soldiers, but by all the citizens, who are bound to attend their prince in time of war (*GT* 67–8).

As is made clear in the voyage to Brobdingnag, such an organisation of the state was considered, in the Tory rhetoric of the early eighteenth century, to be infinitely morally superior to a system based on extensive taxation, and the maintenance of a permanent, or 'standing', army. Not only did individuals resent paying hefty taxes towards the upkeep of the court, but they believed that the dependence of the royal establishment on external assistance represented a departure from the ideal of the self-sufficient estate. A king, it was thought, should live within his means like everybody else, and both the court and the government should be able to subsist on the money derived from the extensive crown lands. Their total inability to do so was taken as symptomatic of the way that the polity had been corrupted by the spread of decadence and extravagance.

The luxury which was seen to be creeping through the society of Britain was thought to be sapping the physical strength and moral integrity of the country. Instead of being prepared to stand up and fight for their homeland in times of strife, the people sat at home and paid taxes which were used to maintain a standing army. This was represented as an extremely worrying and dangerous development because it indicated the effeminacy of modern man, and put the safety of the state in the hands of a group of mercenaries who would presumably work for the highest bidder.[4]

So in his initial presentation of the organisation of the Lilliputian court and army, Swift invoked the ideal of the strong, independent polity, in which individual consumption was controlled by the exercise of frugality, and the defence of the realm was in the hands of the citizens. This image of the ideal nation-state was similar to that celebrated in More's *Utopia*, and it even has some connections with the ideas laid out in James Harrington's *Oceana* of 1656. J. G. A. Pocock, in his magisterial account of the development of republican rhetoric, *The Machiavellian Moment*, has indicated the links between eighteenth-century country ideology, and a republican tradition that can be traced through Harrington to Machiavelli.[5] It thus comes as no surprise that a great traditionalist like Swift combines reflections on contemporary politics with references to earlier genres of political and philosophical writing, invoking not only More and Harrington, but also Plato's *Republic*, but always in such a way as to encourage a questioning of the structures of his own society.

The Lilliputian system does not function for long as an image of what the British government is not. For although Gulliver describes his environment in terms and a tone that suggest that all is equally acceptable and admirable, there are some aspects of Lilliputian society that seem less desirable than others. Even quite early on there is evidence of corruption in the administration of Lilliput, for the Imperial proclamation banning all those who have already beheld Gulliver from approaching his house, unless they have a licence from the court, was, we are told, a means 'whereby the Secretaries of State got considerable fees' (*GT* 67). Moreover, although the Lilliputian court eventually decides to make provision for Gulliver's upkeep, this is only after extensive discussion of ways in which they might get rid of him (*ibid.*).

We are increasingly shown a Lilliput that is far from ideal – that is despotic, arbitrary and ungrateful, and ruled by a clique of courtiers. It is, in fact, the very reverse of the system celebrated in Tory rhetoric, and can be taken as a parodic representation of the ills identified by the country party within the eighteenth-century political system. But this is not what Gulliver tells us. He keeps up the character of a simple seaman, and continues to present his tale with an appearance of gullible ingenuousness. It is thus incumbent on us, as readers, to provide the moral and political gloss that will enable us to identify how the satire is working, and the recognition of this role entails a simultaneous recognition that Gulliver cannot be the model of narrative authority that was constructed at the start of the text. He is not the educated gentleman whose knowledge of the world will guide us towards a 'correct' moral interpretation of his experiences. He is the mouthpiece of an ironic narrative which depends for its construction on the participation of an educated reader, so that Gulliver increasingly becomes a subject, as much as the originator, of the narrative.

This process is dramatised through the incorporation of the inventory of the contents of Gulliver's pockets. This document is not by, but about, Gulliver, couched in a jargon that is at once official and anthropological. It indicates the unhealthy obsession with security that characterises the Lilliputian state, but it also turns the text on the narrator and his things, in a way that gives ample scope for comedy. The reader enjoys the fun of trying to guess what the various objects really are, and the presentation of the familiar through an unfamiliar perspective serves to satirise the nature of European society – in the description of the watch as 'the god that he worships' for example (*GT* 70), but also in the exploitation of that interest in classification and taxonomy which Foucault identified as characteristic of the eighteenth century.

The narrative's ironic objectification of Gulliver is reinforced by the news of the 'little necessaries' (*GT* 69) which he concealed from the Lilliputians, to wit 'a pair of spectacles (which I sometimes use for the weakness of mine eyes)' and 'a pocket perspective' (*GT* 73). A perspective was a telescope, through which things appear larger, or, if you look through the wrong end, smaller than they are in reality. The reference to the weakness of Gulliver's eyes, and his need for corrective spectacles, signals the danger for the reader inherent in over-reliance on the vision of this myopic hero.

Pat Rogers has suggested that in Swift's day the wearing of glasses was associated with studiousness and perceptiveness, rather than the opposite, and that 'the glasses represent visual overdevelopment, hypertrophy of the sight'.[6] Yet although Rogers provides an exceptionally perceptive and even hyper-trophic reading of the use of sight in *Gulliver's Travels*, it is important to bear in mind that for most of the book Gulliver's glasses are not on his nose but in his pocket. They are brought out at significant moments. But it is equally significant that most of the time he wears them not.

The searching of Gulliver's pockets is followed by a classic passage of Swiftian comedy in the presentation of the Lilliputian diversions of rope dancing and 'leaping and creeping' (*GT* 75). The portrayal of rope dancing as a method for deciding between candidates for government office provides a general satire on the flexibility and dexterous footwork that were required to get and maintain office in the early eighteenth century. There is a comic ludicrousness, but also a bizarre appropriateness, in the mental picture of leading politicians doing somersaults, and bending over backwards, in order to stay in power, as Swift literalises the figurative language of political dexterity. As John Traugott has suggested, much of the power of the satire derives from the fact that the 'diversions' of leaping and creeping draw on our memory of childhood games, but the charm derived from such associations is juxtaposed with reminders that the games are all part of a hateful and dangerous political system.[7] Swift exploits the similarities between childhood games and political games in order to show up the childishness of politics, but also, more importantly, to highlight the absence of childish inno-cence in political machinations.

A number of critics in the eighteenth century as well as the twentieth century have detected more specific targets for the satire of this passage, and in particular Robert Walpole has been widely identified with Flimnap, and a variety of readings have been given of the incident with the king's cushion. The search for direct references of this kind has been stimulated by the fact that the portrayal of blue, red and green ribbons as the reward for the exercise of leaping and creeping is clearly intended to mock the British Orders of the Garter, the Bath and the Thistle, which were presented to those members of the court who had ingratiated themselves with the king.

Yet the attempts to scour *Gulliver's Travels* for specific political targets has been vigorously attacked by F. P. Lock, who sees the passages of direct satire as occasional blemishes marring Swift's general technique:

> For much of the book, Swift seems intent on a satire unlimited in its application by time or place, on the nature of man, society, and political activity. Yet this satire is occasionally disfigured by temporary, topical, allusions and teasingly opaque allegories.[8]

Moreover much of the direct satire is found in the Faulkner edition, rather than in the first, Motte edition. Lock provides a convincing argument against the conventional belief that these passages were suppressed by Motte because of his worries over political censorship, and 'restored' to the Faulkner text, and suggests that they must be seen instead as later revisions. Thus Swift 'allowed *Gulliver's Travels* to contain a number of inappositely specific hits at the Walpole regime. And when he came to revise his manuscript, instead of weeding them out he allowed a few more to creep in.'[9]

Lock's account provides a clear and convincing challenge to many of the long-established interpretations of the 'political message' of *Gulliver's Travels*, but at the same time his work is informed by an aesthetic privileging of the general over the particular which I find rather troubling. While his reading has been vital in reinvigorating the study of the politics of *Gulliver's Travels*, it sometimes falls into the opposite trap to that which catches those critics who attempt to read the text as a single consistent allegory. For the structure of the narrative hinges on the dynamic interplay of particular and general satire. Each informs and underlines the other, and we should not neglect or prioritise either.

The conditions for Gulliver's liberty suggested by Skyresh Bolgolam have provided scope for a number of specific allegorical readings,[10] but the Lilliputian articles also play an important role within the text. For they indicate the nature of the relationship between Gulliver and the Lilliputian people, and therefore influence how we evaluate the words and the actions of the two. The 'instrument' begins with satire on the pretensions of the Lilliputian people, and by implication on the pretensions of courts and monarchs in general, by a high-flown paeon that locates the greatness of the 6-inch prince in his superior size. The Emperor of Lilliput is 'Monarch of all Monarchs, taller than the sons of man; whose feet press down to the centre, and whose head strikes against the sun' (*GT* 79). But the substance of the document that follows this heightist introduction is that the 'Man Mountain' should remain in a condition of virtual servitude. From his initial position as the detached observer of the exemplary polity, Gulliver is increasingly exposed as the gullible victim of an oppressive state. This impression is emphasised by the absence of any acknowledgement of the irony of the Lilliputian position, but also by Gulliver's eager acceptance of his servile condition. Although he recognises that the articles are not entirely honourable, Gulliver swears to them with cheerfulness, and the irony is at his expense when he tells us:

> I made my acknowledgements by prostrating myself at his Majesty's feet: but he commanded me to rise; and after many gracious expressions, which, to avoid the censure of vanity, I shall not repeat, he added, that he hoped I should prove a useful servant, and well deserve all the favours he had already conferred upon me, or might do for the future. (*GT* 80)

The effect of this passage is highly comic, but farcical scenes like this make it difficult for modern readers, imbued with contemporary preoccupations about the function of narrative, to understand those nineteenth-century readings that were based on the assimilation of the perspectives of Swift and Gulliver. Surely only the most enthusiastic adherence to a concept of the authoritative narrative voice could ensure the neglect of the ludic and ludicrous elements of Swift's text? Surely Gulliver is clearly intended to appear a fool? The persistence of the 'straight' reading of *Gulliver's Travels* in the criticism of the Victorian period is striking evidence of the potency of the ideas of narrative that the theorists of the twentieth century have sought to undermine.

The univocal view of the novel was encouraged by the fluid narrative and satiric structure which ensures that sometimes Gulliver *does* work as an apparently reliable narrator, and does function to express a point of view which could be allied to Swift's. Thus, immediately after the scene in which he grovels before the tiny Emperor, Gulliver returns to the role of impartial spectator when he gives a seemingly precise account of the appearance of the metropolis of Mildendo. This description is, however, curtailed by Gulliver's assurance that he will shortly be publishing a full history of Lilliput. The reader is brought back from the activities of Gulliver the traveller, to the persona of Gulliver the hack writer, anxious to plug his forthcoming book.

The presentation of the Lilliputian parties epitomises the way that *Gulliver's Travels* combines particular and general satire, for while the *Tramecksan* and *Slamecksan* can be identified as general types,[11] it seems inevitable that these types would have been related by Swift's contemporaries to the parties existing in eighteenth-century Britain, the Whigs and Tories. Moreover the way in which *Gulliver's Travels* manifests the difference between the two groups would have had a particular relevance to the debates of the early eighteenth century. In locating the distinction between *Tramecksan* and *Slamecksan* in the height of their heels, *Gulliver's Travels* implied that party divisions were entirely petty, for from Gulliver's height, and with Gulliver's eyesight, the difference in shoes would be virtually indistinguishable. As a result, the passage serves to endorse the Tory rhetoric which denied the existence of any ideological differences, and decried faction as the product of corruption and the spread of political self-interest. The parties of Lilliput undermine the stability of the state, and therefore render it more vulnerable to foreign attack.

There is similar condemnation of the triviality of religious differences and dogma in the portrayal of the Big-Endian and Small-Endian controversy. The conventional interpretation of the allegory is that it represents the upheavals of the seventeenth century, with the execution of Charles I and the deposing of James II, as the consequence of a debate between Catholics and Protestants that was entirely specious, and fuelled by the traditionally hostile French. The assimilation of religious belief with ideas of egg etiquette was seized upon by critics of the late eighteenth and nineteenth centuries, as a manifestation of Swift's irreligious disposition, and cited as evidence that his career within the Anglican clergy was purely the product of mercenary and highly hypocritical ambition. Yet it would appear from other writings of Swift's, and in particular his *Sermons*, as well as from his activities as Dean of St. Patrick's Cathedral, Dublin, that he was not only a committed Christian, but a violent partisan of the Anglican establishment.

This suggests that it might be necessary to look rather more closely at the egg allegory of *Gulliver's Travels*, in order to ascertain whether there is any divergence between the novel's representation of religion, and Swift's activities as a professional cleric. There can, however, be no simple assimilation of Gulliver's attitude to the Lilliputian egg-crackers, with Swift's attitude to religious difference. Even though Gulliver appears to function in this passage as a fairly reliable narrator, his role is very different from that of Dr Jonathan Swift, polemical defender of the Anglican Church. Unlike Swift, Gulliver is both culturally and physically distanced from the debates which he describes. He is a stranger in Lilliput, with no understanding of the history and ideological significance of the Big-Endian and Little-Endian controversy. He neither analyses nor comments on its history or meaning, but merely records the account that is given by Reldressal.

Reldressal describes the dispute between Blefescu and

Lilliput, and within the Lilliputian state, in terms of overt ceremonial differences. In the same way, the distinction between
Protestants and Catholics in eighteenth-century Britain would
have been most obviously characterised in terms of ritual, and
in particular in terms of the debate over transubstantiation.
For while the Catholics believed that in taking Holy Commun-
ion, the communicant actually partook of the blood and body
of Christ, Protestants held that the bread and wine were only
symbols of Christ. To an impartial spectator, such a dispute
may appear wholly specious, but to the participants it was (and
indeed still is) of fundamental importance, and symbolised a
more general disjunction in the tenets, organisation and
heritage of the reformed and the Catholic Church. The satire
on religion in *Gulliver's Travels* can therefore be seen to mock
not religious doctrine or conviction *per se*, but rather the
ceremonials which are portrayed in *A Tale of a Tub* as
additions or alterations to the basic fabric of Christianity.

Yet even this milder reading of Swift's satiric purpose does
not entirely resolve the divergence between the opinions
implicitly expressed within *Gulliver's Travels*, and the opinions of the work's creator. Throughout his life Swift sought to
safeguard the primacy of the Anglican Church, and to protect
her from both Catholicism and Presbyterianism, and for Swift
as for almost all his contemporaries, the details of ritual and
ceremony were crucial in establishing the differences between
religious groups. Even in *A Tale of a Tub*, the satire is not
equally strong against all the brothers, for the Anglican Martin
is presented as following a middle way between the tyranny of
Catholic Peter, and the disorderly madness of dissenting Jack.
So although there is a level at which the Big-Endian controversy typifies Swift's antipathy to abstruse theological
debate – as also manifested in *A Tale of a Tub* – there is a level
at which it conflicts with his deeply held devotion to Anglican
dogma. Swift the satirist articulates a rather different view of
the world from that which motivated Swift the private
individual, or Swift the professional cleric.

The existence of this disparity should really be inherently

unsurprising, for Swift went to elaborate lengths to dissociate both *A Tale of a Tub* and *Gulliver's Travels* from his persona and authority. The sentiments expressed in each are mediated by the character and perceptions of the fictitious narrator, but, perhaps more importantly, they are also moderated by the conventions of their literary form. The genre of the early eighteenth-century novel was not as well suited to the presentation of detailed and partisan arguments in favour of particular political or religious groupings, as it was to the conveyance of general moral themes. The writer of a novel, through the process of assuming a fictitious voice, inevitably distanced her or himself from the entrenched position from which s/he conducted the debates of everyday life. So just as Gulliver looked down on the people of Lilliput, and could present their customs without the influence of passion and prejudice, so Swift could look down on the world of his fiction, and present the religious debates of his time from a wider, more general and more liberal perspective from that which he adopted in *A Tale of a Tub*, or in those forms of writing that assumed a more engaged and committed voice. This is not to say that the opinions expressed within *Gulliver's Travels* cannot be construed as political propaganda, but the effect of the propaganda is subtilised by the fact that it is diffused through a fictional context, and often adopts the guise of general moral truth – as in the case of the condemnation of party.

In the voyage to Lilliput, however, Gulliver is far from being a touchstone of moral values, because having presented the history of the factions and divisions of the kingdom, with all their apparent triviality, he goes on to embrace the cause of the Lilliputians, in their pointless war with Blefescu. Instead of his size enabling him to put the ambitions of the Lilliputians in perspective, it merely helps him to make a decisive contribution to the war effort. Gulliver is the secret weapon which will realise all the Emperor's imperialistic aspirations. Yet it is clear that Gulliver is not himself invulnerable, for as he is tying up the Blefescudian fleet he is showered by thousands of arrows. He tells us:

> My greatest apprehension was for mine eyes, which I should infallibly have lost, if I had not suddenly thought of an expedient. I kept among other necessaries a pair of spectacles in a private pocket, which, as I observed before, had scaped the Emperor's searchers. These I took out and fastened as strongly as I could upon my nose, and thus armed went on boldly with my work in spite of the enemy's arrows, many of which struck against the glasses of my spectacles, but without any other effect, further than a little to discompose them. (*GT* 87)

This reminder of Gulliver's shortsightedness emphasises his foolishness in getting involved in the war in the first place. But it is his myopia that, through necessitating glasses, saves him from blindness at the hands of the Blefescudians.

The threat to Gulliver's sight serves as a reminder of the importance of keeping one's eyes open, and looking out for danger. It is therefore ironic that half-way back across the channel, when out of the range of the Blefescudian archers, Gulliver stops to take off his glasses. He does not use them when in Lilliput, and so does not perceive the true nature of that country, and the extent of the danger he is in. Indeed, Gulliver is shown to be blinded not by the arrows of Blefescu, but by the court honours of Lilliput, and it is his failure to perceive the threat posed by involvement in this notoriously cut-throat and unstable world that turns out to be his undoing.

Yet for all Gulliver's naive delight in receiving the title of *Nardac*, he does retain some integrity, and argues against the tyrannical ambitions of the Lilliputian Emperor. When required by his Majesty to bring about the total humiliation of the Blefescudians, and the reduction of their kingdom to a province, Gulliver 'endeavoured to divert him from this design, by many arguments drawn from the topics of policy as well as justice: and . . . plainly protested that [he] would never be an instrument of bringing a free and brave people into slavery' (*GT* 89).

In the political reading of *Gulliver's Travels*, this incident deals with the signing of the Treaty of Utrecht, in April 1713. This treaty brought to an end the War of the Spanish Succession, and was the product of secret negotiations between

France and the Tory administration. Robert Harley (Earl of Oxford) and Henry St John (Viscount Bolingbroke) saw no profit in the continuance of the war, which they did not believe they could win outright, and which anyway was tending to increase the prestige of the Whig hero, the Duke of Marlborough. The commercial interest, however, was anxious that the war be fought to the bitter end, in order to bring about the complete destruction of France's foreign trade. When, therefore, the treaty was found to be rather more favourable to the French than might have been expected from the military situation, there was a considerable outcry against the Tories, who were suspected of treasonable collusion with the enemy. The Emperor of Lilliput's desire to carry the war to the utmost extremity, and to bring the Blefescudians to their knees, recalls the Whig attitude to France, which is characterised not as bold nationalism, but as an ignoble and despotic wish for the destruction of 'a Free and Brave People'.[12]

In addition to this political reference, the passage has a crucial importance within the narrative, for it reinforces our idea of Gulliver as the naturally moral man, who can be used to measure the limitations of those around him. Moreover the portrayal of Gulliver's integrity emphasises our sense of the ingratitude of the Lilliputian court, as they gradually turn against their saviour. Indeed, so striking is this ingratitude, that it is even recognised by Gulliver himself, who now begins 'to conceive some imperfect idea of Courts and Ministers' (*GT* 90).

Chapter Five ends with an incident of a more ambivalent character – both morally and allegorically. This is the scene in which Gulliver pisses out the fire in the Lilliputian palace. Arthur Case suggested that Gulliver's action was an allegory of the Tories' negotiations with France prior to the signing of the Treaty of Utrecht, for both acts were technically illegal, but could be seen as necessary for the preservation of the state. Moreover the indecency of Gulliver's method of aiding the Emperor is identified by Case as peculiarly appropriate, since Harley was dismissed by the dying Queen Anne on account of the impropriety of his personal behaviour, as well as his action in supporting an unpopular treaty.[13] But on the whole this interpretation has not been widely shared, perhaps in part because of Case's tendency to interpret almost anything as an allegory of the signing of the Treaty of Utrecht. A more popular theory is that Gulliver's diuresis symbolises Swift's own action in publishing *A Tale of a Tub*.

Although intended as a satire on the misuse of religion, *A Tale of a Tub* was read by many as an attack on the Anglican Church, and it was said that the devout and highly orthodox Queen Anne was particularly offended. Swift always believed that this was why he was never awarded the church preferments which in his own opinion he richly deserved (although Irvin Ehrenpreis's monumental biography *Swift: The man, his works and the age* argues that there is no reason to believe that Swift's expectations were at all reasonable or well-founded).[14] The reaction, or over-reaction, of the Empress of Lilliput can therefore be taken to represent the ingratitude of the Queen's response to Swift's honest attempt to defend and aid her church.

Yet this reading conceals the ambivalent character of Gulliver's action. For although Gulliver saves the Lilliputian palace from fire, he does so not only by breaking the law, but also by causing – as any user of public telephone boxes will confirm – a rather unsavoury form of pollution. It is a question of out of the frying pan and into the urinal, and although the reader may be struck by the Empress's ingratitude, I do not think that s/he can avoid sympathising to some extent with her reluctance to re-enter the royal apartments. If Gulliver's micturation is intended to represent Swift's publication of *A Tale of a Tub*, there appears to be a suggestion that the *Tale* was, if not inherently wrong, at least an inappropriate or unfortunate means of achieving the desired objective, although its use may have been justified by the fact that it was the only thing to hand at the time.

Gulliver's action was not, however, unprecedented. It can be seen as part of the comic repertoire associated with the use of a giant protagonist, for Rabelais' Gargantua, on a visit to Paris 'undid his magnificent codpiece and, bringing out his john-thomas, pissed on [the Parisians] so fiercely that he drowned two hundred and sixty thousand, four hundred and eighteen persons, not counting the women and small children'.[15] There is a childish pride in Gulliver's account of how he 'voided in such a quantity, and applied so well to the proper places, that in three minutes the fire was wholly extinguished' (*GT* 92) so that we are taken right back to the playground. But the Rabelaisian comedy of the jokes about the implications of Gulliver's size is juxtaposed with invocations of the excremental vision, in the representation of the 'abhorrence' of the Empress at Gulliver's act.

This incident is followed by a chapter devoted to a description of the manners and customs of the Lilliputian people, the main import of which is revealed in Gulliver's remark that 'there are some laws and customs in this Empire very peculiar, and if they were not so directly contrary to those of my own dear country, I should be tempted to say a little in their justification' (*GT* 94). Lilliput is once again going to be used to fulfil an exemplary function, and highlight the limitations of the British system. Thus we are told of the advantages of having rewards as well as punishments in the administration of justice, and the tolerance of fraud, corruption and ingratitude within Britain is identified as a practical weakness, as well as a moral failing. The science of government is seen in Lilliput as relatively straightforward, based on certain fundamental moral principles, and dependent on religious faith. The implication is that the needless complexity of the executive, legislative and judicial institutions of Britain help to ensure that the country is vulnerable to the predations of the cunning and corrupt.

The idealisation of the organisation of Lilliput is assimilated to the negative tone of the earlier account on the grounds that:

> In relating these and the following laws, I would only be understood to mean the original institutions, and not the most scandalous corruptions into which these people are fallen by the

degenerate nature of man. For as to that infamous practice of acquiring great employments by dancing on the ropes, or badges of favour and distinction by leaping over sticks, and creeping under them, the reader is to observe, that they were first introduced by the grandfather of the Emperor now reigning, and grew to the present height by the gradual increase of party and faction. (*GT* 96)

The pure constitution and institutions of Lilliput have degenerated over the past century, and have been rendered faulty by corrupt administration. So the original legal and political philosophy serves as an example that shows up the failings of the less perfect British polity, while the actual administration of Lilliput forms both a paradigm of corrupt government, and an allegory of recent events.

As well as making possible this kind of satiric flexibility, the portrayal of the decline of political integrity in Lilliput symbolises the Tory model of British history. A basically sound constitution is shown to have been rendered corrupt by maladministration, and in particular by the canker of faction. This indicates the belief that decay was only introduced over the past century ('by the grandfather of the Emperor now reigning') but also the extent of the emphasis on the need for virtuous monarchs and administrators, as well as a sound constitution, within the state. The voyage to Brobdingnag was to expand on the way that the great and good king could spread a benevolent influence through the country, and ameliorate a potentially faulty system.

The account of the Lilliputian manners and customs is followed by a description of Gulliver's way of living on the island, and the narrative voice embraces the position of freak or spectacle, in dwelling on how his great eating feats were watched by the Emperor and his family. Yet Gulliver's naivety is also exposed, for while he seeks to impress the watching courtiers, by eating even more than usual, he actually undermines his own position, by fuelling the anxiety about how the Lilliputian Treasury will be able to cope with supporting such a voracious guest. Indeed, at this point the ever-hungry

Gulliver may symbolise the standing army, which, in times of peace, did nothing but eat the country out of house and home, and form a tremendous drain on the taxpayers. Despite the fact that the Emperor maintains his court largely on the income from the crown lands, by the end of the war with Blefescu the Lilliputian economy is in a parlous condition similar to that which critics claimed Britain was in at the end of the War of the Spanish Succession. Flimnap complains:

> that he was forced to take up money at great discount; that Exchequer bills would not circulate under nine per cent below par; that I had cost his Majesty above a million and a half of *sprugs* (their greatest gold coin, about the bigness of a spangle); and upon the whole, that it would be advisable in the Emperor to take the first fair occasion of dismissing me. (*GT* 101)

This appeal precedes a very curious passage, which has puzzled many critics, in which Gulliver seeks to deny the suggestion that he had an affair with the Treasurer's wife. It seems likely that this was intended in part as a satire on Sir Robert Walpole and his wife, whose 'open marriage' was notorious in the eighteenth century. But it is also a manifestation of Swift's delight in the ludicrous, conjuring up images that suited the often bawdy and ribald taste of his age with, once again, invocations of Rabelais. The scandalmongers of Lilliput, Clustril and Drunlo, are not deterred by even the most blatant biological facts, and we might infer that the British gossips were equally cavalier.

In chapter seven of the voyage to Lilliput, Gulliver's affairs reach crisis point, as he is impeached by the Council of Lilliput. The incorporation into the narrative of the articles of impeachment, like the earlier inclusion of the list of Gulliver's belongings, and the statement of the conditions for his liberty, represents the exploration and exploitation of a type of writing, or discourse, very different from the form of the novel. The abstruse grammatical constructions and phraseology of legal documents are satirised, and instead of being the presenter and controller of the text, Gulliver becomes the object, whose actions are discussed and condemned.

The legalistic jargon serves to highlight the injustice of Gulliver's trial. For whatever the worthy principles behind the Lilliputian judicial system, the fact of the matter is that Gulliver is sentenced unheard and unrepresented 'without the *formal proofs required by the strict letter of the law*' (*GT* 108). The vindictive brutality of the Lilliputians is emphasised by the commutation of the punishment from immediate execution, to blinding followed by slow starvation. This reminds us of Samson, that other great strongman, who was blinded by the Philistines, and treated as a spectacle. Samson brings the house down on his persecutors. Gulliver decides against such action, but his reasoning on the subject of whether or not he should exact revenge manifests that strange blend of honest virtue and vain inanity that is the hallmark of his character. 'While I had liberty', he muses:

> The whole strength of that Empire could hardly subdue me, and I might easily with stones pelt the metropolis to pieces; but I soon rejected that project with horror, by remembring the oath I had made to the Emperor, the favours I received from him, and the high title of *Nardac* he conferred upon me. Neither had I so soon learned the gratitude of courtiers, to persuade myself that his Majesty's *present severities acquitted me of all past obligations.* (*GT* 109–10)

The juxtaposition of Gulliver's genuine gratitude and humanity, with his credulous pride in the title of *Nardac*, is at once comic and poignant. Gulliver believes in honorific courtly titles, while he rejects the moral values that form the basis of life at court. This position was to undergo considerable modification, however, in the course of Gulliver's second voyage.

3

Looking Up: Brobdingnag

Despite the fact that at the end of the voyage to Lilliput Gulliver had exposed his rather flourishing material condition, and had identified his subsequent voyage as a consequence not of any financial necessity, but of his 'insatiable desire of seeing foreign countries' (*GT* 117), the voyage to Brobdingnag begins with Gulliver denying any kind of responsibility for his decision to go back to sea. Instead of representing himself as a dedicated explorer, he paints a picture of a rather helpless and passive figure 'condemned by Nature and Fortune to an active and restless life' (*GT* 121) and unable rather than unwilling to resist his destiny.

So Gulliver sets sail in the aptly named *Adventure*, and chapter one begins with a catalogue of exotic places, metero-logical phenomena and nautical terms highly reminiscent of the classic travel narrative. We are also provided with a map, as we are at the start of each of the voyages, showing the location of the Brobdingnagian peninsula. This helps to provide an air of verisimilitude, and may be seen as a further contribution to the satire on the travel fiction genre, but it also serves a more symbolic function. For at the time when Swift was writing, cartographic knowledge was still very vague. Many parts of the British Isles, let alone more distant shores, remained unmapped – it would be another hundred years before Swift's native land would be systematically charted by the Ordnance Survey. Yet from the seventeenth century, cart-ographers like Nicholas Sanson and Gulliver's 'worthy friend' (*GT* 333) Herman Moll had sought to construct increasingly accurate maps of the world, and this process was inextricably bound to the process of colonial expansion.

As the European powers spread their spheres of economic influence, they became anxious to become acquainted with the appearance of the countries into which they were moving, but also to fix and appropriate the terms in which those countries were to be described. The process of mapping goes hand in hand with the process of renaming places and countries which is a characteristic feature of colonialism. By naming a place and mapping it you make it your own, and negate the claims and the cultural identity of those already there. Gulliver's mapping can be seen as an incorporation into the satire of a textual manifestation of that system of colonial appropriation which he attacks at the end of the book. Yet it is significant that although Gulliver translates the names of the places he visits, he does not rename them. There is no Queen Anne Island, New Dublin, or St Patrick's Town. *Gulliver's Travels* can be seen to provide a reorientation of the conventions of the discourses of colonial exploitation, through their emphasis on the accept-ance of indigenous cultures. This, however, is a perspective that is only acquired by Gulliver in the course of his travels. His function and outlook in Brobdingnag are very different.

As he cowers amidst the enormous stalks of barley, Gulliver looks back with a misplaced nostalgia to Lilliput, 'whose inhabitants looked upon me as the greatest prodigy that ever appeared in the world' (*GT* 125) and laments that 'as human creatures are observed to be more savage and cruel in pro-portion to their bulk, what could I expect but to be a morsel in the mouth of the first among these enormous barbarians who should happen to seize me?' (*GT* 125). Such a conclusion comes across as particularly odd, given the revelation of the savage barbarity of the diminutive Lilliputians, and we are not surprised to find out later that Gulliver has misjudged the giant Brobdingnagians, who, on the whole, treat him pretty well. He then moves on to more general philosophical speculations which satirise the eighteenth-century interest in epistemology. Gulliver develops the rather obvious premise that 'nothing is great or little otherwise than by comparison' (*GT* 125) to suggest that the world may contain an infinite succession of races, each one-twelfth the size of the last. Every country may have a Brobdingnag and a Lilliput somewhere in the world.

This comic image dramatises the ideas of philosophers such as George Berkeley on the subject of the relativity of concepts of size, and the whole presentation of little and big, Lilliput and Brobdingnag, may be seen to satirise the over-simplistic empiricism propagated by adherents of John Locke's philosophy of perception. Gulliver's is a world in which we cannot believe our eyes – we cannot assume that our senses convey an accurate notion of the nature of reality, and meaning has to be apprehended with reference to pre-existent moral codes. As a result, the philosophy embodied in the narrative structure of *Gulliver's Travels* can be seen to accord with more traditional epistemological ideas, rather than the increasingly popular empiricism.

But Swift's use of size also has a moral dimension, for greatness and littleness were often used in the eighteenth century to describe spiritual as well as physical capacity. Gulliver's identification with races of different scales can give him the ability to evaluate the virtues and vices of his society. How will our ideas of 'human greatness' stand up, when scrutinised from the Brobdingnagian perspective?

At the start of Gulliver's adventures in Brobdingnag, however, the narrative is preoccupied not so much with moral issues, as with the basic practicalities of the size difference, and as in the opening of the voyage to Lilliput, we are encouraged to look through Gulliver's eyes at his environment. From this point of view, the greatness of the Brobdingnagians does not appear as moral strength but rather is identified with the negative ideas associated with the concept of grossness. Despite the hospitality of the farmer's family, Gulliver cannot help being horrified by their enormous bodies – as in the scene in which he encounters the monstrous, 6-foot-high breast – and to Gulliver the giants' skins appear rough and coarse, where the Lilliputians' skins were fine and delicate. Yet at the same time Gulliver's diminutive stature is represented as itself rather revolting, for Gulliver is consistently associated with various forms of vermin. The farm worker picks him up as one would 'a small dangerous animal' (*GT* 125), while Gulliver worries 'that he would dash me against the ground, as we usually do any little hateful animal' (*GT* 126). At the sight of Gulliver the farmer's wife 'screamed and ran back as women in England do at the sight of a toad or a spider' (*GT* 127), and the actions of the farmer's youngest son are explained by reference to 'how mischievous all children among us naturally are to sparrows, rabbits, young kittens, and puppy dogs' (*GT* 129).

The use of negative images in association with either extreme of physical size reinforces the sense of disgust at the human form that is invoked at various points throughout Swift's writing, and is emphasised by the scatalogical element of the satire. Aldous Huxley saw this as the essential motive impulse behind Swift's writing, suggesting that 'Swift's greatness lies in the intensity, the almost insane violence of that "hatred of the bowels" which is the essence of his misanthropy and which underlines the whole of his work.'[1] Carole Fabricant has stressed the importance of 'excremental reality' as well as 'excremental vision', for Swift inhabited a landscape in which human waste products were virtually omnipresent.[2] But Swift's use of references to the processes and products of defecation has struck generations of readers as more than merely a reflection of the inadequate sanitary arrangements of Ireland. The detailed account of Gulliver's toilet arrangements given in the voyage to Lilliput (*GT* 64) may have been justified on the grounds that some explanation was needed for what might otherwise have appeared an insuperable public health problem, but no such justification could be offered for the inclusion of a similar passage in the voyage to Brobdingnag.

The recurrent scatalogical references manifest Swift's conception of the inherent bathos of the human body. The need to 'disburthen' ourselves provides a constant reminder of physicality which will deflate our intellectual pretensions, and highlight the distinction between our spiritual and philosophical aspirations and our material reality. Swift manifests an acute sense of this disjunction, and the reminders of the necessity of defecation provide a satire on Gulliver the individual, but also a warning to philosophers in general. Thus the account of how Gulliver 'discharged the necessities of nature' behind a sorrel leaf is followed by a passage which highlights the significance of this excremental reference:

> I hope the gentle reader will excuse me for dwelling on these and the like particulars, which however insignificant they may appear to grovelling vulgar minds, yet will certainly help a philosopher to enlarge his thoughts and imagination, and apply them to the benefit of public as well as private life, which was my sole design in presenting this and other accounts of my travels to the world; wherein I have been chiefly studious of truth, without affecting any ornaments of learning or of style. (*GT* 133)

In suggesting that the contemplation of his faeces will help to expand the mind of the philosopher, Gulliver draws attention to the artificial separation of mind and body that characterises contemporary philosophical speculation. For while the incongruity of his words satirises Gulliver's rather anal concept of what philosophy should be about, it also mocks the way that the realms of thought and imagination are conceived in isolation from other human functions. Thus Gulliver's words may be taken as serious, in that the references to the inescapable facts of physicality may bring the philosophers back down to earth, and encourage them to apply their thoughts to the practical issues of the public welfare.

At the same time, Gulliver's preoccupation with the minutiae of his voyage, and the concept of narrative authenticity that leads him to recount every detail, are mocked in the account of how:

> The whole scene of this voyage made so strong an impression on my mind, and is so deeply fixed in my memory, that in committing it to paper I did not omit one material circumstance: however, upon a strict review, I blotted out several passages of less moment which were in my first copy, for fear of being censured as tedious and trifling, whereof travellers are often, perhaps not without justice, accused. (*GT* 133)

Gulliver initially wrote down everything, and then took out the less important passages, so that there must originally have been incidents that were *more* 'tedious and trifling' than the account of his bowel movements.

Of course, in part this passage satirises the rather inclusive style of writing that characterised the travel fiction genre, but to many contemporary readers it was this obsession with domestic minutiae that, as much as the obscenity, led to the classification of *Gulliver's Travels* as 'low'. At a time when the novel was only just becoming established as a respectable literary form, the critics tended to favour those works or passages that dealt with grand moral and political themes, and looked down on the preoccupation with verisimilitude (such as is found in the writings of Defoe) as part of a humbler, lower-class tradition of prose fiction, associated with the popular stories propagated in broadsheets and ballads. Thus in the 'Account and Abstract' of *Gulliver's Travels*, published in Abel Boyer's *Political State of Great Britain*, Boyer lamented that 'it were to be wish'd the Author had not follow'd *Rabelais* so close, in some filthy, and obscene Descriptions; nor dwelt so long as he has done, on some mean, minute, and trivial subjects, unworthy the Dignity of a *grand Satyrist*.'[3] It may be this concept of what is fitting the dignity of fiction that Gulliver is satirising in his reference to how he has cut down and edited his travels.

Gulliver's account of the details of his life at the Brobding-nagian farmer's continues with his description of his bed, his 'little nurse', his shirts and so on. This is followed by the scene in which the shortsighted and bespectacled Gulliver entertains himself at the sight of a visitor wearing glasses, whose 'eyes appeared like the full moon shining into a chamber of two windows' (*GT* 135). Gulliver's lack of courtesy is rewarded when the tables are turned, for the visitor recommends that Gulliver should himself become a 'public spectacle' (*GT* 135).

Gulliver is to be shown round the country, just as he had previously shown the Blefescudian cows and sheep – and would have done the natives also, had he been allowed. Yet even before his first appearance at the local town, Gulliver seems, in some respects, to have embraced the role of oddity or spectacle, and to have abandoned any sense of being a self-respecting individual. As in Lilliput, Gulliver turns the act of eating into a performance, which gives 'exceeding delight' to his giant hosts (*GT* 128), and his acceptance of his status as a child, toy or pet is revealed in the complacence with which he refers to his nursemaid, to his appellation 'grildrig' or manikin, to his 'leading strings' (that is, his reins) and to the use he made of the clothes and furniture of Glumdalclitch's dolls.

On his arrival at court Gulliver shows that since his departure from Lilliput he has lost none of his servile sycophancy, for he uses his basic grasp of the Brobdingnagian language to address the queen as 'the Ornament of Nature, the Darling of the World, the Delight of her Subjects, the Phoenix of the Creation' (*GT* 141). In doing so he satirises the insincere hyperbole that characterises court language, but he also demonstrates his own fawning insincerity. He is then handed over for examination by the great scholars attending the court, who eventually agree that he must be a '*lusus naturae*' – a freak of nature. Such a conclusion, reached after extensive empirical observation, mocks the pretensions of scientists who seek to explain the workings of the natural world. For in the face of a phenomenon that does not fit in with their preconceived ideas, the scholars make no attempt to revise their thinking, but only produce a meaningless formula that dismisses the phenomenon as an exception. The professors of Europe no longer rely on the supernatural to explain the apparently inexplicable, but this does not mean that the theories they advance are any more logical or scientific than those of their forebears. They, like the Brobdingnagians, have developed the concept of the '*lusus naturae*' as a 'wonderful solution of all difficulties, to the unspeakable advancement of human knowledge' (*GT* 143).

For the King of Brobdingnag Gulliver functions to provide the moral lesson that is enforced by the use of scale in *Gulliver's Travels* as a whole. The diminutive Gulliver, with his thoughtless pride, represents for the Brobdingnagian monarch an embodiment of human littleness, and the pettiness of both the rewards and the disputes of politics:

> He observed how contemptible a thing was human grandeur, which could be mimicked by such diminutive insects as I: And yet, said he, I dare engage, these creatures have their titles and distinctions of honour; they contrive little nests and burrows, that they call houses and cities; they make a figure in dress and equipage; they love, they fight, they dispute, they cheat, they betray. (*GT* 146)

Even as he speaks Gulliver provides an illustration of the potency of national prejudice, for although he has previously described what in Swift's time would have been seen as the rather less favourable aspects of the British polity – that is our 'wars by land, . . . our schisms in religion, and parties in the state' (*GT* 146) – he is none the less fired with indignation 'to hear our noble country, the Mistress of Arts and Arms, the Scourge of France, the Arbitress of Europe, the Seat of Virtue, Piety, Honour and Truth, the Pride and Envy of the World, so contemptuously treated' (*GT* 146).

In this respect, Gulliver's behaviour in Brobdingnag is rather different from his behaviour in Lilliput. For while in the first voyage Gulliver made various references to his fondness for his own country, at the same time he became a staunch Lilliputian nationalist. Despite being increasingly shabbily treated, he clearly identified himself wholeheartedly with the interests of his hosts, as when he compared the Lilliputian with the Blefescudian wine, claiming that 'ours is esteemed the better sort' (*GT* 92). In Brobdingnag, on the other hand, there is no such assimilation. Gulliver is always conscious of his role as foreigner, and judges the Brobdingnagian culture and polity from a strictly British perspective. Yet while Gulliver remains aloof from the politics, he increasingly identifies himself with the size of the Brobdingnagians. The giants become the norm, and he the deviant, to the extent that he is reduced to the level of laughing at his own reflection (*GT* 146). And while Gulliver is uniquely able to appreciate the danger of the various scrapes he gets into, he none the less shares some of the mirth of the mighty onlookers.

The second book of *Gulliver's Travels* therefore has a rather different satirical function from the first. The Lilliputian court and monarch were respectively an example to, and a parody of, the British government, and Gulliver's failure to signal any consciousness of these conflicting purposes ensured that his status fluctuated with the changing role of his hosts. When he praised those aspects of the Lilliputian polity that provided a favourable contrast with the British system, he came across as a reliable and moral guide. When his praises were directed to those aspects that formed a thinly veiled allegory of the failures and corruptions of the Whigs, he came across as a complete idiot.

In Brobdingnag Gulliver is more consistent, since his advocacy of the British system ensures that he is an idiot most of the time. Instead of recognising the strengths of the Brobdingnagian constitution, and looking down with a critical eye on the corruptions of his country, Gulliver maintains the smallness of mind characteristic of narrow nationalism. But while he rejects the political views of the king, he attempts to assume the physical perspective of the Brobdingnagians, mocking the diminutive stature of his countrymen. Thus Gulliver's problem is that he confuses moral and physical greatness, and his laughable celebration of the latter highlights the extent of his failure to distinguish the former.

There are a number of points in the voyage, however, when Gulliver departs from the automatic equation of size and desirability, finding, as the King of Brobdingnag found with the stray whale, that 'the bigness disgusted him' (*GT* 150–1). He is horrified by the sight of the giant beggars, with their spots, cancers and lice, and the shock of this encounter undermines the strength of Gulliver's identification with the Brobdingnagian perspective. He reverts to the European point of view, becoming the spectator rather than the spectacle, judging the beggars against his own norm, rather than seeing himself as at variance with the standards of others (*GT* 151–2).

A similar distaste is manifested in the scene with the Maids of Honour. Gulliver is knocked out by their smell, disgusted by their nakedness and horrified by the capacity of their bladders. This is a bit of a turnaround, given that in the first voyage there was a note of pride in his account of the 'great astonishment' inspired in the Lilliputian people at the sight of him 'making water . . . very plentifully' (*GT* 60). The odoriferous Maids do not serve to highlight the superior delicacy and fragrance of European ladies, for on the contrary, 'those illustrious persons were no more disagreeable to their lovers, or to each other, than people of the same quality are with us in England' (*GT* 157). The giant bodies expose in gigantic detail the noxious physicality which is shown to be part and parcel of human existence, but which is not usually recognised.

The abhorrence expressed towards Maids of Honour ensured that this scene enjoyed considerable notoriety immediately after the publication of *Gulliver's Travels*, as society gossips speculated on what incidents in Swift's life might have stimulated his animus against court ladies. But the scene is rather more double-edged than this reading suggests, for its exposition of the ugliness of the giant Brobdingnagians is juxtaposed with a display of the utter ridiculousness of the tiny Gulliver, as he is made to ride on the nipples of 'a pleasant frolicsome girl', and to perform 'many other tricks wherein the reader will excuse me for not being over-particular' (*GT* 158) – from which we might infer that he was used as a human dildo. While the inflated bodies of the Brobdingnagians reveal the grossness of humanity, the antics of the squeaking Gulliver simultaneously suggest an idea of littleness and laughable powerlessness.

This accords with the general terms of Swift's reflections on human physicality, but it also suggests a particular fascination with the female body, and its relationship to perceptions of the male self. We have already heard in Lilliput about suggestions that Gulliver had an improper association with one of the tiny court ladies, but here the idea of the disjunction between male and female is turned around. An underlying sense of the vulnerability of the male is exploited in the portrayal of Gulliver as sexual plaything, no longer the proactive giant, but the tool of dominant women. The Maids of Honour are in a position of power, by virtue of their size, but they are also essentially childish. It is their 'frolicsome' games that pose the greatest threat to the sensibilities of the prurient Gulliver.

This ambivalent attitude towards female sexuality is further developed in the celebration of the central relationship between Gulliver and Glumdalclitch – the giant little girl. Gulliver's authority as the older man is constantly undermined by the limitations imposed on him by his size. Glumdalclitch is young and unsophisticated, but the consequence of this is a rather disconcerting freedom from the customary restraints that control male/female relations. The very fact of her youth serves to challenge Gulliver's integrity and sense of self, for she regards him not as a figure of authority or even an equal, but rather as a toy. The vulnerable child is also a dominant and domineering figure, practising the role of nursemaid on her captive subject male, and enforcing a rigorous regime. The relationship between Gulliver and Glumdalclitch can therefore be read as a paradigmatic embodiment of Swift's perception of sexual difference. The use of giant women and tiny men can be seen as a comic dramatisation of an underlying anxiety that beneath the frolicsome innocence of the girl child may lie a desire to dominate, and reorient conventional power relationships, as well as a fear that the games and 'tricks' might be sexual in origin, foreshadowing the games of the adult world.

But the mockery of Gulliver is also important in emphasising the political message of the book. For the more foolish and ludicrous Gulliver becomes, the easier it is to recognise the pettiness and smallmindedness of the narrow nationalism he articulates. This is important, because Swift was writing at a time when love of country tended to be seen – as it often is today – as an unquestionable virtue. *Gulliver's Travels* has to display the vicious potential of nationalistic sentiment, when it involves an adherence to decadent or corrupt institutions.

The relevance of this to the European context is displayed in the focal scene of book two, in which Gulliver has to describe the British polity to the King of Brobdingnag. The terms in which he confronts this task do not bode well for his cause, for Gulliver appeals to the 'courteous reader' to 'imagine . . . how often I then wished for the tongue of Demosthenes or Cicero, that might have enabled me to celebrate the praises of my own dear native country in a style equal to its merits and felicity' (*GT* 167). It could be argued that a truly happy and virtuous country should not need a great orator to sing its praises. The homely testament of personal experience should do. But the irony is rather more subtle than this, for Demosthenes and Cicero are famed not for their eulogies on their countries, but for 'philippic' orations, in which they castigated the corruption and decadence of Athens and Rome respectively, in order to urge a reformation. Both orators are regarded as great patriots, but they are wise and visionary patriots, rather than blind nationalists, and their love of country forces them to speak out against the degeneration they identify as liable to lead to the collapse of the state.

Ironically, Gulliver's words will also serve as a philippic oration, for the terms of his eulogy, combined with his truthful answers to the pertinent questions of the king, constitute an indictment of the manifold abuses of the British legal and political systems. The structure of the irony is at first straightforward. Gulliver heaps wholly undeserved praise on his country's administration, presenting an idealised view of the polity that brings home to the reader the very un-ideal character of the way that things actually work. So the behaviour of members of the House of Lords is satirised by Gulliver's description of Peers of the Realm as 'the ornament and bulwark of the kingdom, worthy followers of their most renowned ancestors, whose honour had been the reward of the virtue, from which their posterity were never once known to degenerate' (*GT* 167–8).

The satire becomes a little more complex once the king begins his cross-examination. The reader is expected to supply answers to enquiries such as 'what qualifications were necessary in those who are to be created new Lords?', reinforcing the impression of the unsavoury nature of the administration. And as the king picks out the logical inconsistencies of Gulliver's account, our hero is increasingly exposed as a highly partial and unreliable witness. His affection for his 'beloved country' is simultaneously displayed as misplaced, and shown to be the cause of considerable deviation from the truth, for which he proclaims an 'extreme love'. The satire is at the expense of the corruptions of the British polity, but also of the blind and slavish patriotism that causes its adherents to distort reality.

The terms of the implicit critique of the political system are very revealing of Swift's ideological preoccupations, for the King of Brobdingnag raises those issues, of party, faction and corruption, that were central to the Tory, or country party, critique of the political system. This critique was given one of its clearest formulations in Henry St John's *Dissertation upon Parties* of 1734. This argues that the taxation which had resulted from the wars of William III and Anne had generated increased patronage, which, by perverting the integrity of politicians, had undermined the independence of parliament, and so thwarted the primary purpose of the 1688 Revolution. St John proclaims that:

> It is time for every man who is desirous to preserve the British constitution, and to preserve it secure, to contribute all he can to prevent the ill-effects of that new Influence and Power which have gained strength in every reign since the Revolution; of those means of corruption that may be employed one time or another on the part of the crown, and that proneness to corruption on the part of the people, that hath been long growing and still grows.[4]

The King of Brobdingnag's query whether promotion to the nobility might not sometimes be the consequence not so much of natural virtue, but rather of 'the humour of the Prince, a sum of money to a Court lady, or a Prime Minister, or a design of strengthening a party opposite to the public interest' invokes the spectres of patronage and its associate, corruption, which were conventionally seen to have undermined the integrity of the state. By assimilating the overt bribery of 'a sum of money to a Court lady' with the desire of strengthening a party, the passage indicates the extent to which faction and party were regarded as both inherently undesirable, and a product of the development of the patronage system. The king's references to the Tory image of the corrupt state are contrasted with Gulliver's naive vision of the polity, which confuses the ideas and the theory behind the constitution with how things actually work in practice.

Thus Gulliver represents the House of Commons as '*freely* picked and culled out by the people themselves, for their great abilities and love of their country' (*GT* 168), while the king queries whether they may not sometimes have a view to 'refunding themselves for the trouble they were at, by sacrificing the public good to the designs of a weak and vicious prince, in conjunction with a corrupted ministry' (*GT* 170). In addition, the king enquires into the process by which the commoners are elected, asking 'whether, a stranger with a strong purse might not influence the vulgar voters to choose him before their own landlord, or the most considerable gentleman in the neighbourhood' (*GT* 169). To the Tory way of thinking it was right and proper that voters should elect their own landlord, or the richest man in the area. The very fact that an individual possessed land and wealth was thought to mean that he would naturally be able to understand the needs and interests of the community, because he had a vested interest in the maintenance of stability, national prosperity and the status quo. Corruption was identified not with the tendency of landlords to force their neighbours and tenants to elect them, but with anything that prevented such elections from taking place. As a result the Tory critique of parliament of the early eighteenth century was very different from the radical critique of the mid-nineteenth century. The Victorian reformers sought to overthrow the natural association of political power with landed wealth that was fundamental to the country-party rhetoric of the eighteenth century, and seen as a remnant of the 'Ancient Constitution' of the land.

One of the fundamental principles of Tory philosophy in the early eighteenth century was the belief that the state should be defended by a citizen militia rather than a standing army. The former was seen as more noble, more manly and more reliable than the latter, for every militiaman was fighting for his hearth and home, rather than for a daily wage. As the king suggests 'a private man's house might . . . better be defended by himself, his children, and family, than by half-a-dozen rascals picked up at a venture in the streets, for small wages, who might get an hundred times more by cutting their throats' (*GT* 171). Moreover the opposition to the standing army was tied up with the opposition to the national debt, and to all the institutions associated with deficit financing. The standing army was thought to be, like Gulliver in Lilliput, a voracious monster, causing the imposition of punitive taxes, living off the backs of the productive classes, but also spawning an enormous and seemingly unproductive financial system, that sprang up to service the vast debts incurred in maintaining the often idle ranks.[5] Furthermore the existence of a professional soldiery was identified as liable to encourage unnecessary conflict, and particular political impetus was given to this argument at a time when the Tory apologists were finding they had to defend the hasty conclusion of the War of the Spanish Succession.

The Tory argument that the standing army was both unnatural and undesirable is emphasised by the king's surprise at Gulliver's account. Like so many citizens of eighteenth-century Britain (or even of twentieth-century Britain come to that), the king is 'at a loss how a kingdom could run out of its estates like a private person' (*GT* 171). He believes that 'we must be a quarrelsome people, or live among very bad neighbours' to be engaged in 'such chargeable and extensive wars' (*GT* 171). As to the process of Imperial expansion so dear to the hearts of the mercantile sectors of the eighteenth-century populace, he cannot understand 'what business we had out of our own islands, unless upon the score of trade or treaty, or to defend the coasts with our fleet' (*GT* 171).

In his attitude to not only the financial system and foreign policy, but also political faction and religious dissent (which may be privately practised but not propagated) the king is a staunch exponent of Tory rhetoric. He points out what to Swift and his associates were the major failings of the British political system, but in Britain as in Lilliput it is the administration rather than the constitution that is identified as most at fault. The king is able to discern 'some lines of an institution, which in its original might have been tolerable, but these half erased, and the rest wholly blurred and blotted by corruptions' (*GT* 172). The final conclusion, that the bulk of British natives are 'the most pernicious race of little odious vermin that Nature ever suffered to crawl upon the surface of the earth' (*GT* 173), is given comic emphasis by Gulliver's assurance that:

> I artfully eluded many of his questions, and gave to every point a more favourable turn by many degrees than the strictness of truth would allow. For, I have always borne that laudable partiality to my own country, which Dionysius Halicarnassensis with so much justice recommends to an historian. (*GT* 173)

None the less Gulliver is anxious to return to his society, and to his 'domestic pledges', and this homesickness comes across as laudable love of country and paternal affection. Gulliver manifests an interestingly ambivalent attitude to his position in Brobdingnag. On a personal level, he seems entirely happy to adopt the role of freak, oddity or spectacle. This is perhaps understandable, for he 'was indeed treated with much kindness'. He 'was the favourite of a great King and Queen, and the delight of the whole Court' (*GT* 180). But when he considers the possibility of begetting a whole race of little people, who will fulfil the same function as himself, as standing jokes and pets of the wealthy, he is filled with horror and disgust. Gulliver is able to conceive the position of his imaginary progeny with more impartiality than he can summon up in relation to himself. A situation which circumstances have rendered necessary to be borne by an individual is identified as unendurable or inconceivable for a people. This projection into posterity therefore reinforces Gulliver's sense that his position 'ill became the dignity of human kind', and fires his desire to 'be among people with whom [he] could converse upon even terms, and [to] walk about the streets and fields without fear of being trod to death like a frog or a young puppy' (*GT* 180).

His escape therefore comes as a blessed release, despite a few anxious moments when the box is carried away by the eagle. But when Gulliver is once again amongst his own kind, his behaviour rather belies the previous protestations of his desire to leave the land of the giants. Gulliver is confounded 'at the sight of so many pygmies' (*GT* 185) and goes round shouting at the top of his voice. Far from missing the company of his fellow creatures, Gulliver appears to have adopted the perspective of the Brobdingnagians, so that he looks down on the sailors around him as 'little contemptible creatures' (*GT* 189) and enjoys considerable mirth at the sight of 'dishes of the size of a silver threepence, a leg of pork hardly a mouthful, and a cup not so big as a nutshell' (*GT* 189–90).

This propensity becomes quite bizarre on his return to his family. Given that this followed a sea voyage via Australia you would have thought that he would have had time to adjust, but instead he rides home, shouting to all and sundry to get out of his way, bending double to get in at his own front door, and attempting to pick up his daughter between finger and thumb. This is intended as 'an instance of the great power of habit and prejudice' (*GT* 191) and the ludicrousness of Gulliver's behaviour forms an apt conclusion to a voyage in which much of the satire has hinged on Gulliver's foolish and blind prejudice for his own country. Instead of adopting the enlightened philosophical and political perspective of his hosts, Gulliver has adopted their physical perspective. His foolishness in scorning the stature of his countrymen is therefore matched by the idiocy of his failure to apprehend with Brobdingnagian eyes the true 'littleness' of British institutions.

Combined with all the analysis of perspective in this final chapter is a comical satire on the travel-writing genre, for

Captain Wilcocks' request that Gulliver should publish an account of his adventures, is met with the reply:

> That I thought we were already overstocked with books of travels: that nothing could now pass which was not extraordinary, wherein I doubted some authors less consulted truth than their own vanity or interest, or the diversion of ignorant readers. That my story could contain little besides common events, without those ornamental descriptions of strange plants, trees, birds, and other animals, or the barbarous customs and idolatry of savage people, with which most writers abound. However, I thanked him for his good opinion, and promised to take the matter into my thoughts. (*GT* 189)

Swift is clearly mocking the exaggerations and excesses that characterised travellers' tales, but in stressing that his story is not about the 'barbarous customs and idolatry of savage people' but contains only 'common events', Swift may also be making reference to the symbolic function of the text.

The juxtaposition of the giant Brobdingnagians with the diminutive Lilliputians emphasises the way that these characters function in relation to Gulliver as physical embodiments of the literary techniques of meiosis and hyperbole. Just as the literary tropes are employed for satiric effect, so the presentation of tiny and huge societies ostensibly provides a comic commentary on the nature of the British polity. But the concept that ideas of size are entirely relative complicates this simple satiric structure, for if there is an infinite succession of races of different sizes, we cannot necessarily equate the position of Gulliver with a normative controlling perception. It may be Gulliver, and, by implication, we ourselves, who are out of proportion, rather than the races who are supposedly the subjects of the traveller's tale. The articulation of a philosophy prioritising political stability is therefore combined with a fictional structure that is increasingly disorienting, and this process of disorientation is accelerated in the third voyage, when Gulliver actually leaves the ground.

4

Flying Around: Laputa

The satire of book three has been identified with two rather different sources. In their 1937 article 'The Scientific Background of Swift's "Voyage to Laputa"', Marjorie Nicolson and Nora Mohler argued:

> That Swift borrowed for the 'Voyage to Laputa' even more than for the other tales, but that the sources of his borrowings were different. The mathematicians who feared the sun and comet, the projectors of the Grand Academy, the Flying Island – these come to Swift almost entirely from contemporary science. The sources for nearly all the theories of the Laputans and the Balnibarians are to be found in the work of Swift's contemporary scientists, and particularly in the *Philosophical Transactions of the Royal Society.*[1]

More recently, Pat Rogers has challenged this generally accepted interpretation, suggesting that

> The best location for sources and analogues as far as projects go, is not the *Philosophical Transactions* but the columns of the newspapers in the Bubble era and the patent applications of the day. *Gulliver's Travels* was written at a time of exuberant commercial expansion and fertile practical invention. Its cultural matrix can be defined as the Age of Projectors – a bustling, uncerebral world of entrepreneurs and inventors . . . Swift . . . meant to site Lagado nearer Exchange Alley than Gresham College.[2]

But whether the specific satire is derived from the one, the other, or a combination of the two, the basic thrust is the same. The craze for experimentation, in both science and projecting, was associated with an enthusiasm for the new which ran counter to the respect for the old that was a mainstay of Tory political philosophy. The members of the Royal Society, and the projectors of the Bubble era, were supporters of the commercial expansion and exploration that was associated with the colonial and imperialistic aspirations of the Whig administration. It is characteristic of Swift's method that this general trend is attacked in all its multitudinous manifestations. References to contemporary schemes and more general scientific trends are combined and juxtaposed, each serving as an eloquent synecdoche for the broader political movement of progressive forces.

In many ways, Gulliver has, by the third voyage, become an embodiment of the new progressive order. He is an adventurer, unable to rest on his laurels and stay at home with his wife and family, always thirsting to explore new places and see the world. But it is not just his restless spirit that makes him keep returning to sea. He is also motivated by that 'prospect of advantage' that is so influential with Mrs Gulliver (*GT* 195). Gulliver progresses from being a ship's surgeon (book one), to being a trader in a small way (book two), to become a captain's assistant (book three) and finally, in book four, a ship's captain. From being the son of a member of the landed gentry at the start of book one, Gulliver has been transformed into a self-made man, an entrepreneur with no ties to the land, who symbolises the perpetual quest for new goods and new markets that was central to the plans for economic expansion of many of the Whiggish thinkers of the early eighteenth century.

Gulliver represents the proto-imperialistic, trading interest, as is evident in the opening chapter of book three, but his *Travels* also parody the enthusiasm for exploration that characterised many of the scientists of his day. Gulliver brings together, as trader and travel-writer, the realms of commercial expansion and scientific advance. His restless energy epitomises the drive towards the new that lies behind both forms of 'progress'. When Gulliver's character and integrity are explored and undermined, it is at once mercantilism and new science that are put under the microscope, as Swift displays what he believes to be the consequences of the general betrayal of traditional values and principles. Both science and commerce are identified and attacked as the product of a particular political ethos.

But the fact that Gulliver is motivated by a thirst for novelty, innovation and knowledge does not stop him from serving, in Swift's flexible satiric form, as a touchstone of normality against which the excesses of others can be measured. In his own society, Gulliver has quite a turn for science and mathematics, but in Laputa he becomes the man in the street, mystified by the abstruse pedantry of the philosophers. Likewise, Gulliver is a representative of a modern, progressive commercial society, but in his encounter with the Japanese pirates he provides a critique of the code of morality associated with a commercial economy.

The Japanese were regarded in the eighteenth century as quintessentially brutal pagans, yet the pirate captain is portrayed in *Gulliver's Travels* as far more humane and charitable than the Dutchman. Holland was Protestant, and in alliance with England against the French, but it was also seen as the greatest trading nation in the world, wholly imbued with commercial values, and devoted to the pursuit of profit. In representing the Dutchman as vengeful and inhuman, Gulliver may be attacking the Dutch nation for their conduct in the Grand Alliance, but he may also be indicating the kind of behaviour to be expected from the people of a country that was thought to draw its morality from the balance sheet, and to emphasise commercial exigency above all else. In other words, he may symbolise not the behaviour of the Dutch in particular, but rather the behaviour of the inhabitants of trading nations in general.

Once Gulliver has been set adrift in his canoe he sails between various uninhabited islands for almost a week before being hoisted onto the flying island. This lonely sojourn provokes an uncharacteristic despondency in the normally ebullient adventurer, but the melancholy does not take the form of Crusoe-like reflections on the spiritual condition of man. Rather, it is based on an anxiety for his personal safety that is assuaged as soon as he reaches Laputa. This practicality indicates the extent to which Gulliver differs from Defoe's hero, but also from his Laputian hosts. The Gulliver of book three is interested in the real and concrete, the day-to-day details of existence. Progress for him is measurable in standards of living and material benefits. In contrast, the Laputians are preoccupied with abstract issues and theoretical speculations. Gulliver as travel-writer embodies the contemporary interest in ethnography, anthropology and the expansion of knowledge, and so may be allied to the progressive, anti-traditional forces in society. But he is also the 'good science' of practical improvement that may be contrasted with the abstruse and irrelevant science that is identified as highly deleterious to society.

The contrast between the down-to-earth Gulliver and the head-in-the-clouds Laputians is made manifest by the use of the satiric device that is a particular feature of *Gulliver's Travels*, by which Swift literalises figurative concepts. The philosophers do not have their feet on the ground; they have their heads in the clouds by virtue of the fact that they live on a flying island. This island defies the kind of cartographic fixing that Gulliver attempts to provide at the start of each of his voyages, and represents at once a triumph of technical ingenuity, and the chimerical, insubstantial and unworldly nature of Laputian learning. As such that satire forms part of a tradition of attacks on abstract theorising which included Samuel Butler, Thomas Shadwell and William King. Even Joseph Addison, who was a devotee of Newtonian science, 'lost no chance for laughter at impractical experimenters and at absent-minded mathematicians who in their preoccupation with one subject forgot the world about them'.[3] Likewise Swift's friend, John Arbuthnot, was keenly interested in many areas of scientific exploration, but none the less joined in the Scriblerian project 'to ridicule all the false tastes in learning'.[4] While the satirical tradition emphasised certain recurrent comic stereotypes, it was not always inherently anti-scientific, but could be adapted to attack the perversion of scientific method and endeavour, by bad scientists, or by commercial or political interest groups.

In Laputa the prioritisation of complex theory over practical method ensures the shoddy construction of Laputian houses, for as Gulliver remarks 'although [the Laputians] are dextrous enough upon a piece of paper in the management of the rule, the pencil and the divider, yet in the common actions and behaviour of life, I have not seen a more clumsy, awkward, and unhandy people' (*GT* 205). As Carole Fabricant has emphasised, the images of a disorganised, badly built and badly maintained country that recur throughout book three of the *Travels* may well have been drawn from the landscape of Swift's native Ireland, where many houses could be found in which 'the walls bevel, without one right angle in any apartment'.[5] The juxtaposition of the actual irregularity and disorder of the Balnibarbian landscape with the obsession with order and precision of the Laputian rulers satirises the unworldliness of these mathematicians, but also suggests a more culpable dereliction of duty. While the social elite speculate and philosophise, the rest of the inhabitants of Laputa or the Balnibarbian mainland seem to live in poverty or squalor, or labour in conditions of servitude as 'flappers' to the philosophical oligarchs.

The Laputian devotion to the study of science and mathematics is the cause of emotional and moral as well as social and practical problems. For the people of the flying island live in perpetual dread that the world will be destroyed by collision with the sun or a comet, or by global cooling caused by a decline in the power of the sun (*GT* 206–7). All these ideas were present in contemporary scientific thought, in the work of Isaac Newton, Robert Hooke, William Derham and Edmund Halley,[6] and had often been satirised by the Scriblerians. But the angst-ridden Laputians do not just mock the millennialist tendencies of particular theories. They also provide a more general attack on the function of science in society. The Brobdingnagian scholars' classification of Gulliver as *lusus naturae* suggested that scientific knowledge and terminology did not necessarily eliminate superstition. In the voyage to Laputa this point is expanded, as Gulliver shows that far from contradicting, science may in fact reinforce irrational fears and anxieties by giving them an apparently rational framework and justification.[7]

Despite the celebratory tone of the account of the operation of the flying island, and the Laputian astronomical discoveries (including the identification of two satellites of Mars, unknown in Europe until 1877), the terms of the portrayal of the benefits of scientific and mathematical progress are ambiguous. The philosophers are credulous and timorous, but also incredibly dull, with no concept of 'imagination, fancy, and invention' (*GT* 206). It is easy to see why their wives get fed up and leave them, to run off with footmen and so on, for although Gulliver declares Laputa to be 'the most delicious spot of ground in the world' (*GT* 208) he too itches to depart, and confines his conversation to 'women, tradesmen, *flappers*, and Court-pages' (*GT* 217) during his two-month stay.

But the society of the flying island is more than just dull. Swift moves beyond the cosy satirical tradition of mocking the quaint absent-mindedness of the dotty professor, to invoke a rather more bitter and serious indictment. Beneath the jocularity of book three are indications of the tyrannical potential of both science itself, and of a society based on an intellectual elite. The squalor and sterility of both Laputa and its subject kingdom, Balnibarbi, demonstrate how knowledge can be misused and abused, as well as misapplied.

This less light-hearted aspect of the satire on science is tied up with the voyage's political dimension, manifested most clearly in the description of the Lindalino rebellion. This passage was not included in the text of *Gulliver's Travels* until 1896 when G. A. Aitken published it as an appendix. In 1899 the four paragraphs were restored to their proper place. As soon as the passage was incorporated it was recognised as an allegory of the battle over Wood's halfpence. In 1722 William Wood, an English iron dealer, characterised by Swift as a 'hardware man'

Gulliver's Travels

and a 'low mechanic', paid the Duchess of Kendal, mistress of George I, £10,000 for a patent to mint 360 tons of halfpence and farthings to the value of £100,800. The existence of such a patent was not in itself unusual, for in the absence of a national mint for Ireland, the Crown regularly permitted private citizens to produce base coins. But it was the excessive quantity of coin allowed by Wood's patent, combined with the very low percentage of copper to be included in each coin, that caused anxiety in Ireland, for as Oliver Ferguson explains in his book *Jonathan Swift and Ireland*: 'Not only did this . . . allow Wood what seemed to the Irish an unreasonably large profit, but the low intrinsic value of his halfpence posed a threat to Ireland's supply of gold and silver.'[8]

The Irish people therefore reacted angrily to the proposals. According to the 'secret history of the event' detailed by William Coxe in his *Memoirs of the Life and Administration of Sir Robert Walpole, Earl of Orford* of 1798, 'the spirit of opposition seized all orders of men, and even many of the king's servants who held the chief places under his administration.'[9] One of the loudest, angriest and wittiest complainants was Jonathan Swift, who, in the persona of a Dublin drapier, published the *Drapier's Letters*, lambasting Wood and the English adminstration, and exhorting the citizens of Ireland to join a boycott of Wood's coin:

> For my own Part, I am already resolved what to do; I have a pretty good Shop of *Irish Stuffs* and *Silks*, and instead of taking Mr. WOODS's bad Copper, I intend to Truck with my Neighbours the BUTCHERS, and *Bakers*, and *Brewers*, and the rest, *Goods for Goods*, and the little *Gold* and *Silver* I have, I will keep by me like my *Heart's Blood* till better Times, or till I am just ready to starve, and then I will buy Mr. WOOD's Money as my Father did the Brass Money in K. JAMES's Time, who could buy *Ten Pound* of it with a *Guinea*, and I hope to get as much for a *Pistole*, and so purchase *Bread* from those who will be such Fools as to sell it me.[10]

Such was the strength and persistence of the protest, and the effectiveness of the boycott, that in August 1725 Wood's patent was withdrawn, to the immense satisfaction of the drapier and his supporters.

Lindalino can therefore be seen to represent Ireland or Dublin, a subject people who successfully fight against the 'great oppressions' of a dominant Imperial power. Laputa represents a brutal and oppressive administration, prevented from destroying its subject peoples not by compassion or humanity, but rather by a self-interested fear of destruction.

In *The Politics of Gulliver's Travels*, F. P. Lock has questioned not only this interpretation of the rebellion, but also the inclusion of the episode in the text at all, suggesting that it was cut from the original edition as a result of a deliberate stylistic decision:

> It is really a rejected idea of Swift's that happens to have been preserved through . . . accident . . . Its narrative mode is quite unsuited to *Gulliver's Travels*. Whatever its precise meaning, it invites detailed allegorical interpretation in a way that most of *Gulliver's Travels* does not.[11]

Yet although Lock's argument for the omission of the passage from the body of the text is convincing, I am not persuaded by the associated stylistic criticisms. As I have already indicated, I see *Gulliver's Travels* as a protean narrative, that unites particular and general satire within an interdependent whole, rather than a general satire that is marred by occasional particular 'lapses'. The description of the Lindalino rebellion, following the account of rebellions in general, functions as an exemplum to develop the implications of the preceding passage. And although we are not able to say with certainty what particular features, such as the 'strong pointed rock' (*GT* 215), represent within the allegorical structure, it seems unlikely that Swift's contemporaries could have read of the tensions between a dominant imperial power and a neighbouring subject kingdom without thinking of England and Ireland. Such an association could only be reinforced by the knowledge that the work was written by the author of the *Drapier's Letters*. The Lindalinian rebellion is therefore important within the text in displaying that rejection of colonial injustice which was to be such an important feature of the second half of the *Travels*. The subject peoples are revealed not as abject dependants, but as courageous and ingenious, while the Lindalinians are barbarously tyrannical.

Yet ironically the dominance of self-interest on the part of the courtiers, combined with the division of power between the king and his lords, ensures that the Laputian regime is not as brutal as it might be. For:

> The King would be the most absolute prince in the universe, if he could but prevail on a Ministry to join with him; but these having their estates below on the continent, and considering that the office of a favourite hath a very uncertain tenure, would never consent to the enslaving their country. (*GT* 214)

Moreover the ministers are reluctant to destroy the cities of the mainland by dropping the island upon them, because 'as it would render them odious to the people, so it would be a great damage to their own estates, that lie all below, for the island is the King's demesne' (*GT* 214). Once again, the parallels with Anglo-Irish relations seem obvious, but there is also a more general political point.

The stability of the Laputian government is located in property ownership, for the very fact that the ministers and courtiers are endowed with wealth in land ensures that they have a personal, vested interest in the protection of the public interest of Balnibarbi. Because they have a private source of income, they are unlikely to be tempted to risk everything in a bid for supreme power. The salvation of the Laputian administration is thus identified as that emphasis on property-ownership, combined with the separation of power between the king and his ministers, which Swift and his associates saw as the fundamental cornerstone of the British system of government. The Laputian court is ruthless and oppressive, but it is by no means as bad as it would be if it were not grounded in the ownership of land. The implication is that the same is true of Britain.

This serves to reinforce the argument that Laputa does not alway represent England, for it is often used to symbolise the

English court, which hangs over and dominates not only Ireland, but the whole of the British Isles.[12] Such a reading helps to illuminate the satire of the flying island, for the picture of the impractical and incompetent philosophers makes much more sense as an image of life in the rarified realm of a court, than it does as a representation of the English people as a whole. The court of George I is portrayed as distant from the rest of the nation, floating about in a world of its own, and imposing arbitrary exactions. The cacophonous concert in Laputa mocked the Hanoverian monarch's well-known predilection for music, and in suggesting that all other arts were neglected in the court, Swift seems to be endorsing a prevalent Tory complaint about the decline of literary patronage after the death of Queen Anne.

But as has already been suggested, the interest in science of the inhabitants of Laputa also had a wider political significance, representing what the Tory thinkers believed to be a potentially disastrous disrespect for established traditions and ways of doing things, in the face of an enormous investment of academic and financial interest in novelty and innovation. The early eighteenth century witnessed a craze for invention and experiment, and the court as well as the financial institutions bristled with projectors who were prepared to invest their money in new products. In such an environment, many of the projects were, as Pat Rogers has indicated, either pointless or unsuccessful or both, and many of the projectors lost money and face.[13] But the heady atmosphere also encouraged considerable advances in scientific knowledge, and the development of numerous production processes and techniques.

The enthusiasm for new science was associated with Whiggish politics, and also with a brand of Anglicanism known as 'latitudinarianism'. This was a form of religion which sought to reconcile the desire to live virtuously with the desire to make a profit within a commercial system. It presented what Margaret Jacob, in her fascinating account of the political significance of Newtonianism, *The Newtonians and the English Revolution*, has described as 'a Christianized capitalism, an ethic for self-interest resting upon the providential order in the world political and natural'.[14] Scientists such as Robert Boyle were prominent latitudinarians, and noted latitudinarian theologians such as Archbishop Tillotson and Benjamin Hoadly showed considerable interest in scientific discoveries. So Swift's antipathy to scientific theorising may in part have been motivated by his adherence to the High-Church party which was implacably opposed to the growth of latitudinarianism within the Anglican establishment. The portrayal of the fear of the end of the world may therefore refer not just to the superstitious potential of science, but also to the latitudinarian use of Newtonian physics to construct a model of how the destruction of the world would come about if there were no moral reformation.

This suggests that book three of the *Travels* is not the amorphous and incongruous hotchpotch that has often been supposed. The voyage is not only based on real experiments, but, perhaps more importantly, is thoroughly integrated into the thematic and allegorical structure of the rest of the book. The picture of Laputian society condenses and elides the political and theological arguments that crop up throughout the *Travels* by presenting a specific attack on the Whiggish court, and the modern latitudinarian tendency in religion, as well as providing a general satire on the prevalent obsession with everything new.

In Laputa as in Lilliput there are various references to the difficult relationship between King George I and the Prince of Wales. In Laputa this latter is represented as the 'great Lord at Court, nearly related to the King, and for that reason alone used with respect' (*GT* 218). As one of the few court allies of the disgruntled Tories, the Prince of Wales is celebrated as the only courteous and intellectually curious character on the flying island. Elsewhere the more indirect satirical passages are interspersed with more obvious references to the British court, as when the account of the Lindalinian rebellion (or before its restoration, the account of rebellions in general) is suddenly followed by the statement that 'By a fundamental law of this realm, neither the King nor either of his two elder sons are permitted to leave the island, nor the Queen till she is past child-bearing' (*GT* 217). To Swift's contemporaries this would have been an inescapable allusion to the Act of Settlement of 1701, which stipulated that the king could only leave the country with the express permission of parliament.

Once Gulliver leaves the court for Balnibarbi, the implications for the state of the projecting mentality are fully revealed. The Balnibarians 'walked fast, looked wild, their eyes fixed, and were generally in rags' and even the well-travelled Gulliver 'never knew a soil so unhappily cultivated, houses so ill-contrived and so ruinous, or a people whose countenances and habit expressed so much misery and want' (*GT* 219). In contrast to this barren landscape is the estate of the benevolent Lord Munodi, 'a most beautiful country' with 'farmers' houses at small distances, neatly built, the fields enclosed, containing vineyards, corn-grounds and meadows'. Gulliver has never seen 'a more delightful prospect'.

Numerous suggestions have been made about who formed the model for Munodi, but in this passage the identity of the particular individual is far less important than the general import of the satire. Whether he be Bolingbroke,[15] Lord Middleton[16] or Oxford,[17] Munodi represents a paternalistic Tory squire, who has held out against the mania for improvement, and maintained the traditional management practices of the past. His name, a contraction of 'mundum odi' – 'I hate the world' – indicates the misanthropy that is seen as an almost inevitable consequence of such a common-sense attitude. For a rejection of the prevalent fads and fancies seems to require a total or partial withdrawal from a world in which those who refuse to conform to convention are 'looked on with an eye of contempt and ill-will' (*GT* 222).

But probably the most famous passage of the whole of the third voyage, and that which has commonly been taken to epitomise Swift's attitude to science, is that in which Gulliver visits the Grand Academy of Lagado. In his 'Account and Abstract' of *Gulliver's Travels*, Abel Boyer explains that the Academy 'is intended to expose and ridicule the *Follies* and *Whimsies* of *Cabalists*, *Virtuosi*, *Chymists*, *Empyricks*, *Whistonians*, *Desaguillerians*, and in short, of all *Crack-brained Experimental Philosophers*'. He adds, however, that the 'Satyr is so be daub'd and clogg'd with *filthy*, and *loathsom* Images, that it cannot but be *fastidious* and *fulsom*, to persons of a *delicate Taste*, and *Nice Breeding*'.[18]

As Nicolson and Mohler have shown, the experiments of the projectors represent only a *reductio ad absurdam* of real experiments performed by members of the Royal Society. Their purpose is to ridicule the belief, articulated in Francis Bacon's *Advancement of Learning* of 1605 and *The Great Instauration*, that scientific knowledge should not proceed on the basis of a priori theories, but instead should be located in a body of empirical data. Scientists should accumulate as much information as possible about the physical world, through observation and experiment, and this information might ultimately lead to the construction of general scientific laws.

Bacon's posthumous *New Atlantis* presented an image of a publicly financed scientific institution, known as 'Solomon's House', which would discover the 'knowledge of causes and secret motions of things; and the enlarging of the bounds of Human Empire, to the effecting of all things possible'.[19] This utopian vision was very influential with the early architects of the Royal Society, after its founding in 1660, and the influence of Baconian methodology is indicated by the inclusion of Bacon's portrait as a frontispiece to Thomas Sprat's *History of the Royal Society* (1667) with the title 'artium instaurator'. Amongst the triumphs of the experimental method were the works of Sir Isaac Newton, and in particular the *Philosophiae Naturalis Principia Mathematica*. As the preface to this work explains, the adherents of experimental philosophy: 'assume nothing as a principle, that is not proven by phenomena . . . From some select phenomena they deduce by analysis the forces of Nature and the more simple laws of forces; and from thence by synthesis show the constitution of the rest.'[20] But as well as encouraging scientific innovation, the Baconian bent of seventeenth- and eighteenth-century science also led to much mindless and pointless experimentation, and the indiscriminate accumulation of information.

Both Bacon and Sprat stress the need to refine and improve not only knowledge and experimentation, but also the language in which scientific findings are expressed, or, in Sprat's words, 'the manner of their *Discourse*'. This was of the utmost importance to the Royal Society, for 'unless they had been very watchful to keep [it] in due temper, the whole spirit and vigour of their *Design*, had been soon eaten out, by the luxury and redundance of *speech*'.[21] It is therefore this preoccupation with the need to communicate ideas directly, without the 'superfluity' of 'eloquence' that stimulates Swift's satire on the 'school of languages', with its project 'to shorten discourse by cutting polysyllables into one, and leaving out verbs and participles, because in reality all things imaginable are but nouns', and the even more ludicrous project 'for entirely abolishing all words whatsoever' (*GT* 230).

The catalogue of the crazy schemes of the various departments of the Academy is interrupted by the rather poignant satire of the account of the unhappy political projectors who are:

> Proposing schemes for persuading monarchs to choose favourites upon the score of their wisdom, capacity and virtue; of teaching ministers to consult the public good; of rewarding merit, great abilities and eminent services; of instructing princes to know their true interest by placing it upon the same foundation with that of their people; of choosing for employments persons qualified to exercise them; with many other wild impossible chimeras, that never entered before into the heart of man to conceive, and confirmed in me the old observation, that there is nothing so extravagant and irrational which some philosophers have not maintained for truth. (*GT* 232)

This satire draws heavily on the conventional Tory critique of the inevitably corrupt nature of courts and politics, but this representation of the image of a moral and healthy polity as some kind of strange and bizarre idea is followed by a return to the satiric method that characterises the rest of the account of the Academy, as Gulliver describes in respectful tones, the ridiculous experiments of the political projectors. The identification of a school of politics within the Academy may refer to the prevalent idea that the theories of new science were applicable to all spheres of human endeavour. Michael Hunter suggests in *Science and Society in Restoration England* that:

> The belief that everything could be reduced to mathematics is characteristic of the thought of the time and it was taken to absurd extremes, as when efforts were made to reduce politics and even morality to geometry: thus the Dublin virtuoso, Samuel Foley, wrote a paper entitled 'Computatio Universalis seu Logica Rerum, Being an Essay attempting in the Geometrical method to Demonstrate a Universal Standard whereby one may judge the real Value of Everything in the World'.[22]

In addition the chapter satirises the vogue for novelty, particularly in the financial sphere, which was thought to characterise political administration. For the new economic systems, and above all the methods for funding the national debt, were viewed with tremendous suspicion by conservative critics of the government, and seen as a way of exploiting the public through a form of political projecting.

The political allegory is developed during Gulliver's visit to the island of Glubbdubdrib, as he conjures up the spirits of the past. For although Gulliver starts by summoning the heroes of classical antiquity, these figures were highly politically resonant in the very classically based republican rhetoric of the early eighteenth century. Brutus and Cato were models of public virtue, whose willingness to sacrifice their private interests for the good of the state was frequently contrasted with the corruption that was identified as inherent in the modern political system. Thus when Gulliver compares the Senate of Rome with a modern parliament 'The first seemed to be an assembly of heroes and demigods; the other a knot of pedlars, pickpockets, highwaymen and bullies' (*GT* 241). In the battle between ancients and moderns that Swift had satirised in *The Battle of the Books*, Gulliver seems firmly on the side of the ancients.

This is evident in the scene in which Gulliver introduces Homer and Aristotle to all their numerous commentators, and the argument of the 'moderns' of the superiority of contemporary science is undermined by the suggestion that the scientific theories of Aristotle, Gassendi, Descartes and Newton are all equally faulty. For Aristotle argues that:

> New systems of nature were but new fashions, which would vary in every age; and even those who pretended to demonstrate them from mathematical principles would flourish but a short period of time, and be out of vogue when that was determined. (*GT* 243)

Once Gulliver starts to call up the figures of recent history the satire becomes more bitterly social and political. The comic references to the predominance of bastardy in the families of courtiers and monarchs are followed by a passionate attack on the injustices of their administrations, and of the historians who have consistently concealed that injustice:

> I found how the world had been misled by prostitute writers, to ascribe the greatest exploits in war to cowards, the wisest counsel to fools, sincerity to flatterers, Roman virtue to betrayers of their country, piety to atheists, chastity to sodomites, truth to informers. How many innocent and excellent persons had been condemned to death or banishment, by the practising of great ministers upon the corruption of judges, and the malice of factions. How many villains had been exalted to the highest places of trust, power, dignity, and profit: how great a share in the motions and events of courts, councils, and senates might be challenged by bawds, whores, pimps, parasites, and buffoons: how low an opinion I had of human wisdom and integrity, when I was truly informed of the springs and motives of great enterprises and revolutions in the world, and of the contemptible accidents to which they owed their success. (*GT* 244)

The cause of this corruption is hinted at in the account of the sea captain who had fought at the battle of Actium. This story is probably an allegory of some eighteenth-century injustice, but even if it is read at face value it has a clear relevance to Swift's time. For the battle of Actium was one of the events which signalled the end of the Roman Republic and the beginning of the Imperial era. It was therefore identified in much of the political rhetoric of the seventeenth and eighteenth centuries as the herald of that moral and social degeneration which marked the movement from a republican government based on public virtue, to an Empire that was increasingly based on decadence and consumption. The decline of the Roman Empire was seen as a direct result of the spread of luxury and private interest and the over-extension of colonial power. The fate of Rome was held up by critics of the commercial economy of Britain as an example of what would happen if getting and spending continued unabated. Thus Gulliver moralises:

> I was surprised to find corruption grown so high and so quick in that Empire, by the force of luxury so lately introduced, which made me less wonder at many parallel cases in other countries, where vices of all kinds have reigned so much longer. (*GT* 247)

This passage is followed by a comparison between the degenerate physique of modern man, and the hale and hearty figure of the stout English yeoman. Here Gulliver draws on that mythology of the farmer as the repository of true, traditional virtue which formed the basis of the association of political power with the ownership of land. The yeomen of Tory rhetoric were 'famous for the simplicity of their manners, diet and dress, for justice in their dealings, for their true spirit of liberty, for their valour and love of their country' (*GT* 247), because the very fact that they owned their own land gave them independence, and an interest in the maintenance of social and political stability. But even these small farmers have succumbed to the national disease of political corruption, and through selling their votes have sacrificed the liberty of their country in the interests of short-term private gain.

The basic cause of this departure from the 'pure native virtues' of the past is indicated in the satire on the Dutch that marks Gulliver's visit to Japan. For as in the encounter with the pirates at the beginning of the voyage, the Dutch traders are portrayed as considerably more brutal and barbarous than the

Japanese, so that once again commercial society is identified as the source of moral depravity. Indeed *Gulliver's Travels* goes so far as to suggest that being from Holland and being Christian are mutually exclusive, for when the supposedly Dutch Gulliver asks permission to be excused the ceremony of trampling on the crucifix:

> The Emperor . . . seemed a little surprised, and said, he believed I was the first of my countrymen who ever made any scruple in this point, and that he began to doubt whether I was a real Hollander or no; but rather suspected I must be a CHRISTIAN. (*GT* 262)

Thus the voyage to Laputa satirises the various features which Swift and his associates believed to be characteristic of contemporary society – its commercialism, its irreligion, the corruption of life at court, the vogue for the new, and the disrespect for the old. This is all articulated within a framework of quite specific satire on people and events of recent history, so that, in eighteenth-century terminology, the work is both 'particular' and 'general'. Nowadays the particular satire has lost much of its immediacy, being comprehensible only through notes and glosses, but the tenor of the general satire is still clearly discernible. Even so, it is important to recognise that the general attack on change was itself related to a particular political perspective. In the eighteenth century, as today, the celebration of the past in comparison to the present inevitably served to attack the current administration – in Swift's case the Whig government of Sir Robert Walpole. This was seen to be becoming increasingly corrupt, tyrannical and arbitrary, and was barely restrained by what the Tories identified as the remnants of the Ancient Constitution, symbolised in the constitutional organisation of Laputa. The dangers of political absolutism are represented in the description of the ceremony of the court of Luggnagg, whereby supplicants are requested by the king to '*lick the dust before his footstool*' (*GT* 249). This represents a deadly extension of the court games of Lilliput, and combines with the evocation of colonial oppression and maladministration in Laputa to provide a resonant warning against tyrannical government and imperialism.

5

Out to Grass:
Houyhnhnmland

If voyage one and voyage three of *Gulliver's Travels* are the books of direct political satire, two and four are the more philosophical sections, for while one and three tend to attack things as they are, two and four deal more with how things might or ought to be. But in the case of book four at least, there is by no means a clear critical consensus over the nature of Swift's ideal. As indicated above, the questions of how we relate to the Houyhnhnms, how we judge their society, and how we interpret Gulliver's peculiar behaviour, have recurred throughout the twentieth century.

One of the most notable features of the opening of the voyage is the extent to which Gulliver is himself the object of the satire. For with reference to the late Captain Pocock we are told:

> He was an honest man, and a good sailor, but a little too positive in his own opinions, which was the cause of his destruction, as it hath been of several others. For if he had followed my advice, he might at this time have been safe at home with his family as well as myself. (*GT* 267)

Given that Gulliver has always been a marked devotee of his own opinion, as was clearly the case in his final dispute with the ill-fated Captain Pocock, this remark comes across as a case of the pot calling the kettle black. Moreover Gulliver's bumptious arrogance seems particularly out of place since his own return to the bosom of his family was by no means a foregone conclusion, and owed far more to good luck than to the judgement of which he boasts. Gulliver is clearly being smug, and we laugh at him for this, but at the same time we know, even if he does not, that pride comes before a fall.

We are not kept long in waiting for the fall. In fact, it comes in the next paragraph, when Gulliver is taken prisoner by his mutineering men, and is then cast away on an unidentified island. As Gulliver sets off up country, trinkets in hand, ready to barter with the 'savages' (*GT* 269), I find that, as a modern reader, I am hoping that his imperialistic pride will be mortified. Lo and behold, it is. The disgust excited by the filthy Yahoos serves to undermine that personal and racial arrogance embodied by Gulliver at the start of this voyage. Gulliver thinks he is so clever and so superior, but he is really only a Yahoo with clothes on. What is more, at first he does not even realise it. His horror at the sight of the Yahoos, and his failure to identify their similarity to himself, emphasise the extent of the blind prejudice that controls our perception of ourselves. Gulliver's self-respect and patriotic fervour can only survive by the suppression of all consciousness of the nature of human physicality. When he is confronted by the Yahoos his reaction is acute: 'Upon the whole, I never beheld in all my travels so disagreeable an animal, nor one against which I naturally conceived so strong an antipathy' (*GT* 270).

This initial antipathy is compounded when Gulliver is caught under a tree full of Yahoos who are determined to shit on his head. The disgust excited by this horrible incident is, and always has been, shared by a considerable proportion of Gulliver's readers. In contrast to the Yahoos, the Houyhnhnms initially come across as gentle and civilised creatures, although the social implications of their dominant position are indicated almost in their first appearance. When the dapple-grey neighs at the retreating Gulliver 'I fancied myself to understand what he meant, whereupon I turned back, and came near him, to expect his farther commands' (*GT* 271). The Houyhnhnms are born to give commands which even civilised Western Yahoos almost instinctively obey.

Gulliver's conscious response to the horses is, however,

rather less deferential, for he is not yet ready to recognise their social superiority, and accept the status of a Yahoo. Working on the thesis that the horses are magicians in disguise, he reverts to the old Imperial stereotype of offering trinkets in return for safe passage (*GT* 272). Once he reaches the house, having jettisoned the magician theory, out come the toys again, in the form of 'two knives, three bracelets of false pearl, a small looking-glass and a bead necklace' (*GT* 274). These, unsurprisingly, cut little ice with the aesthetic horses, so that Gulliver has to abandon the role of patronising colonial trader, and in a short time embraces the position of submissive servant to his Houyhnhnm 'master'.

The scene in which the Houyhnhnms compare Gulliver and the Yahoo indicates not only Gulliver's position within Houyhnhnm society, but also his own idea of his true nature and status. For while the Houyhnhnms are preoccupied with the dissimilarities between the clothed Gulliver and the naked Yahoo, Gulliver is struck by the extent of the resemblance. The secret of his clothes is therefore vital for the initial establishment of his status as a non-Yahoo, but at the same time Gulliver knows that this is a sham. The shoes and clothes provide only a veneer, a false covering that hides the thoroughgoing Yahoo that lurks beneath. As such, Gulliver's clothes symbolise the nature of the 'civilisation' by which he distinguishes himself from the 'savage nations', and all the references to clothing, dressing and undressing reinforce the fact that this is only a thin disguise that can conceal but not alter the bare truth about human nature. This therefore represents a reorientation of the clothing metaphor that is used in *A Tale of a Tub*. For in *A Tale* the clothes are made of good, strong material and are of simple, practical design.[1] They are useful in themselves, but have been cut about and altered by the dictates of fashion. In the *Travels* it is not just fashion that is satirised, but the idea of wearing clothes at all, for this is seen as a sign of decadent effeminacy as well as that human reluctance to embrace the disjunction between our philosophical pretensions and our physical reality which Norman Brown has identified as the key to Swift's 'excremental vision'.[2]

The importance of clothing is comically dramatised in the scene in which Gulliver, while swimming naked in the river, is approached by a female Yahoo and embraced 'after a most fulsome manner' (*GT* 314). This, we are told:

> was matter of diversion to my master and his family, as well as mortification to myself. For now I could no longer deny that I was a real Yahoo in every limb and feature, since the females had a natural propensity to me as one of their own species. (*GT* 315)

In some respects the native Yahoos may be seen as superior to the supposedly civilised Gulliver, for the Yahoos do not seek, through an artificial covering, to deny their natural brutality. They do not try to be something they are not. As such, it does not seem far-fetched to suggest that the Yahoos represent the lower classes, who live in the filth, muck and depravity that is the natural lot of man, while Gulliver symbolises the futile attempts of the social elite to use the false refinements of clothes and manners, and a specious pretence of reason, to hide their connection with the lower orders. Carole Fabricant suggests that:

> In many ways, the depiction of the Yahoos, as Sir Charles Firth noted, recalls the description given by Swift, in prose pamphlets written about the same time, of the people whom he terms 'the savage old Irish'. More broadly, the Yahoos embody characteristics that Swift periodically observed in Irish people as a whole: slovenliness, squalor, and a certain kind of barbarity, paradoxically coexisting with an excessive submissiveness to authority . . . On one level the Yahoos are the Irish as perceived with lofty disdain by a highly cultivated elite who have fully sublimated all biological and emotional urges to higher forms of rational thought and civilized behaviour.[3]

But the contrast is not only between the Yahoos and their 'icily detached colonial masters'.[4] It is also between the brutal but unpretentious Yahoos and the pretensions to civilisation of the sartorial Gulliver. The terms of the portrayal of the Yahoos therefore manifest the ambivalence of Swift's attitude towards the human species. For Swift was caught in a cultural limbo, between the world of London, polite society, with its emphasis on the rational, and the world of eighteenth-century Ireland, in which, as Fabricant has indicated, the physical realities of human existence were all too obvious. Gulliver recognises his image in the Yahoo breed, yet he cannot reconcile himself to the reflection. He aspires to the rational society of his equine hosts, but he cannot ever hope to be like them. In Gulliver's predicament, Swift articulates not only the anxieties resultant from his position as a member of the Anglo-Irish elite, but also the awareness that this engendered of the uncertain status of humanity as a whole.

Although the Yahoos sometimes represent natural, primitive man, unrestrained by social codes, the flexibility of Swift's satire ensures that they sometimes symbolise the corrupt decadence characteristic of an advanced commercial society. In the article of diet they seem to fall into the latter category, for while the Yahoos are greedy carnivores, and stuff themselves with food and intoxicating roots (*GT* 309), the abstemious Gulliver subsists on a diet of bread, milk and herbs. While the Yahoos succumb to a variety of ailments induced by their 'nastiness and greediness', and known by the general name of 'hnea-Yahoo' or 'Yahoo's-evil' (*GT* 309), Gulliver 'never had one hour's sickness' (*GT* 279) while he stayed on the island.

The 'hnea-Yahoo' clearly represents the 'diseases produced by repletion' (*GT* 310) which Swift identifies as epidemic within the luxurious social elite of early eighteenth-century Britain. But at the same time Gulliver is shown to be able to reject the gluttony of the Yahoo nature, and adopt the alimentary frugality that characterises Houyhnhnm-kind. He is and is not a Yahoo, and is able to assume elements of Houyhnhnm morality. This fluidity has served to confound some of the critics of *Gulliver's Travels*, who have sought simple allegorical equations, but it is itself central to an understanding of Swift's narrative and satiric method, and to the role of Gulliver and the reader within the text.

Gulliver moves from being an exemplary human, who can be contrasted with both the native Yahoos and the British society they symbolise, to being the object of the narrative subtext. This ensures that the reading process is not just the passive reception of information, but instead involves the experience of moral, political or philosophical uncertainty, and is essentially disorienting. Reading does not simply enlighten; it enlightens through destabilising perception to induce a radical questioning of what otherwise might be accepted as the eternal verities of the social and mimetic systems. So in a way the experience of uncertainty is the whole point of the book.

From this it might be argued that the critical debate over book four only undermines the impact of this experience. For the hard/soft battle is essentially devoted to establishing whether or not Gulliver's extravagant admiration for the Houyhnhnms is to be taken at face value, and whether we should really see the passionless horses as ideal. Yet the persistence of the hard/soft debate in many ways goes to show that there is no simple reconciliation or negation of the conflicts within the text of *Gulliver's Travels*, and that literary criticism no more deals in certainties than do the literary texts themselves. In fact, far from removing the destabilising impact of works, criticism may reinforce it, by bringing out its extent, implications and reverberations within the narrative.

One of the areas where this has been the case is the analysis of the concept of language in book four. This has been ably elucidated by Michael McKeon, in his epic account of *The Origins of the English Novel*. McKeon notes that although Gulliver is famed for his facility in languages, even he is prepared to admit to having difficulty with the Houyhnhnm tongue:

> At first it appears that this is the result of the primitive state of the Houyhnhnms' understanding, reflected in their regrettable paucity of words and expressions. But it soon becomes clear that what they lack is rather the superfluity of vicious desires that make language obscure and complicated and that are symbolized in the confusion of the Tower of Babel. Ironically it is Houyhnhnm speech that approximates most closely, in *Gulliver's Travels*, a universal language.[5]

Moreover:

> The Houyhnhnms have no 'Occasion to talk of *Lying*, and *false Representation*', not only because their wills are not infected, but because in their speech there is a perfect correspondence and consistency of word and thing. In Houyhnhnmland, the absence of a highly elaborated language is directly analagous to the absence of a highly elaborated economy.[6]

Houyhnhnm speech has a simplicity and expressiveness that is clearly admirable, but as McKeon points out, this purity of language is only possible because of the austere nature of the Houyhnhnm polity. The mistake the projectors of Lagado made was not in believing that a simple language is desirable, for Swift appears to endorse the idea that it is, but rather in believing that language can be taken as an independent variable. Societies have the grammar that they need and deserve, and so a corrupt society will necessarily produce a corrupt tongue. For Gulliver to learn the Houyhnhnm language properly, therefore, he has to unlearn the decadent thinking of Western capitalism. Even once he has mastered the Houyhnhnm tongue, he has the greatest difficulty in communicating the nature of British society to his Houyhnhnm host, 'for their language doth not abound in variety of words, because their wants and passions are fewer than among us' (*GT* 288). As a result Gulliver strives to express himself 'by similitudes', though hampered by the fact that Houyhnhnmland has nothing that is comparable to many of the things or concepts that he wants to communicate (*GT* 289): 'Power, government, war, law, punishment, and a thousand other things had no terms, wherein that language could express them, which made the difficulty almost insuperable to give my master any conception of what I meant' (*GT* 291).

There are few wants, and so few words, in Houyhnhnmland, but in addition it is a place of the here and now. There is no history, only direct oral communication, for 'the inhabitants have not the least idea of books or literature' (*GT* 281). The fact that the Houyhnhnms are illiterate has been taken by some critics as evidence that their society cannot have been seen by a

97

great scribbler like Swift as any kind of ideal utopia. Yet we encounter this statement about the Houyhnhnms in a context which suggests that we are initially intended to take it at face value, and see it as an indication of the admirable simplicity of equine life. It is only later, as the less admirable aspects of Houyhnhnm society emerge, and as Gulliver's reliability as a narrator is progressively undermined, that we may be led to make a retrospective revaluation of the significance of the illiterate nature of Houyhnhnm culture. Reading *Gulliver's Travels* is not a simple progressive process, for the shifts within the narrative structure necessitate repeated revaluations of what has gone before. What means one thing at one point in the book may mean quite another later on. Things that look big in one context come to look small in another, and what at first appears good may later seem less desirable. As the cold and unemotional character of the horses is revealed, our idea of their illiteracy may be revised, to form evidence of a prosaic lack of imagination, rather than an admirable simplicity.

Given the importance and protean nature of perspective within *Gulliver's Travels* there seems no reason to believe that the whole of Houyhnhnm society must be intended as an ideal, simply because the language is celebrated. None the less throughout the Houyhnhnm master's conversations with Gulliver on the nature of the British polity, the simple life of the horses serves as an exemplary model against which the corruptions of decadent commercial society can be measured. This is similar to the satiric technique employed in the voyage to Brobdingnag, and the horror of the Houyhnhnm master is comparable to that of the Brobdingnagian monarch, as he hears of how:

> Difference in opinions hath cost many millions of lives: for instance, whether *flesh* be *bread*, or *bread* be *flesh*; whether the juice of a certain *berry* be *blood* or *wine*; whether *whistling* be a vice or a virtue; whether it be better to *kiss a post*, or throw it into the fire; what is the best colour for a *coat*, whether *black*, *white*, *red* or *grey*; and whether it should be *long* or *short*, *narrow* or *wide*, *dirty* or *clean*. (*GT* 292)

Gulliver's summary of the doctrinal disputes and ceremonial distinctions between the Anglican and Catholic Churches makes them appear as ludicrous as the Lilliputian controversy between Big-Endians and Small-Endians, as well as emphasising sartorial differences similar to those employed in *A Tale of a Tub*. But in the *Tale* the clothing is used metaphorically. Here the satire is based on the presentation of the real structures and customs of European society in terms which sound like a ridiculous allegory.

But much of the effectiveness of the passage comes from a bleaker, less comic, dramatic irony, which draws on our apprehension of the disjunction between Gulliver's expectations, and the reception we predict his words will receive. Gulliver's enthusiastic description of:

> cannons, culverins, muskets, carabines, pistols, bullets, powder, swords, bayonets, battles, sieges, retreats, attacks, undermines, countermines, bombardments, sea-fights; ships sunk with a thousand men, twenty thousand killed on each side; dying groans, limbs flying in the air, smoke, noise, confusion, trampling to death under horses' feet; flight, pursuit, victory; fields strewed with carcasses left for food to dogs, and wolves, and birds of prey; plundering, stripping, ravishing, burning, and destroying (*GT* 294)

is hardly calculated to endear the human race to the seemingly peaceable Houyhnhnms. That Gulliver is still oblivious to this fact is emphasised by his account of how:

> to set forth the valour of my own dear countrymen, I assured him, that I had seen them blow up a hundred enemies at once in a siege, and as many in a ship, and beheld the dead bodies drop down in pieces from the clouds, to the great diversion of all the spectators. (*GT* 294).

So distanced have the readers become from Gulliver at this point that they are able to judge British society from the perspective of the Houyhnhnms. We condemn its irrational and pointless barbarity, and at the same time are faced with the ludicrousness of blind, nationalistic prejudice. As described, the human race is a sorry spectacle, but in a way Gulliver is even worse. It is one thing to hear about wars, death and destruction. It is quite another to hear about these things from someone who glories in them as signs of bravery and intelligence.

Yet despite Gulliver's fondness for 'the dear place of [his] nativity' (*GT* 299) the influence of the Houyhnhnms is such that in the course of his conversations with his master, which take place over more than two years, his account of European society becomes increasingly candid and increasingly critical. For Gulliver confesses that:

> The many virtues of those excellent *quadrupeds*, placed in opposite view to human corruptions, had so far opened my eyes and enlarged my understanding, that I began to view the actions and passions of man in a very different light, and to think the honour of my own kind not worth managing. (*GT* 305)

As a result he gives a none too favourable account of the workings (or otherwise) of the British legal system, and his account of the economic structure draws heavily on the anti-commercial writings of the seventeenth century. These emphasised the use of money, combined with the luxurious consumption of the rich, as the cause of increasing social inequality, in a system in which 'the bulk of our people was forced to live miserably, by labouring every day for small wages to make a few live plentifully' (*GT* 298). The complaint that:

> In order to feed the luxury and intemperance of the males, and the vanity of the females, we sent away the greatest part of our necessary things to other countries, from whence in return we brought the materials of diseases, folly, and vice, to spend among ourselves (*GT* 299)

is typical of the rhetoric which identified luxury as the consumption of foreign goods, and saw domestic goods as inherently healthy and more wholesome.

Gulliver's appraisal of his country continues with descriptions of the gluttony of the people, of medical practices, and of the political system. This 'free representation' is followed by the Houyhnhnms' comments, which reinforce the critique, either directly, through their pertinacity, or sometimes obliquely. For the foolish or irrational character of human behaviour is emphasised by the difficulty experienced by the honest Houyhnhnm in understanding its nature. The bestiality, passion and greed behind various human actions are revealed by displaying their similarity to the behaviour patterns of the Yahoos, and the differences between humans and Houyhnhnms. To modern readers, however, the advantage does not always appear to be on the side of the horses. For:

> Among the Houyhnhnms, the *white*, the *sorrel*, and the *iron-grey* were not so exactly shaped as the *bay*, the *dapple-grey*, and the *black*; nor born with equal talents of mind, or capacity to improve them; and therefore continued always in the condition of servants, without ever aspiring to match out of their own race, which in that country would be reckoned monstrous and unnatural. (*GT* 304)

Nowadays this caste system comes across as horrific. Yet to many of Swift's contemporaries it would have represented an orderly society, in which everyone knew their place. In contrast, European society was often seen as unstable because the development of a commercial economy had ensured that many people within the system did *not* know their place, and were encouraged to rise above their station, even sometimes 'aspiring to match out of their own race'. Swift satirises the British class system on two counts. The first is the fact that the nobility, far from being in any way physically and intellectually superior (as they are in Houyhnhnmland) are, as a consequence of their endemic 'idleness and luxury', 'scrofulous, rickety or deformed', characterised by 'a weak diseased body, a meagre countenance, and sallow complexion'. The second prong of the attack is the reference to that aspect of the behaviour of the nobility which helps to negate the former weakness – that is, the tendency of the wives to 'take care to provide a healthy father among her neighbours or domestics, in order to improve or continue the breed' (*GT* 304). Unlike the mares of Houyhnhnmland, where 'the violation of marriage, or any other unchastity, was never heard of' (*GT* 317), the women of Great Britain not only indulge their '*lewdness*' outside marriage, but do so with members of a lower class or caste.

It is when Gulliver moves from the satire on British society and the description of the Yahoos, to the account of the manners and morals of the Houyhnhnms, that the narrative becomes rather more ambiguous. For a start, what are we to make of the Houyhnhnm adherence to reason? Gulliver tells us:

> It was with extreme difficulty that I could bring my master to understand the meaning of the word *opinion*, or how a point could be disputable; because *Reason* taught us to affirm or deny only where we are certain; and beyond our knowledge we cannot do either. So that controversies, wranglings, disputes, and positiveness in false or dubious propositions are evils unknown among the Houyhnhnms. (*GT* 315)

Given that this occurs within a narrative which has emphasised the importance of variations in perspective in determining how we see things, which has continually exploited differences in point of view, and which avoids any kind of presentation of a single 'right reading' or normative authorial position, can we really take it at face value? Even if we do accept that Houyhnhnm society represents an ideal, is it an ideal that can be transferred to the society of erring disputacious humankind?

There are two basic arguments against the acceptance of the Houyhnhnms as ideal. The first is the simple matter of their unappealing nature. As Kathleen Williams puts it:

> If Swift did intend the Houyhnhnms to stand as an ideal contrast he has badly mismanaged the matter. The Houyhnhnms do not strike the reader as altogether admirable beings; indeed they are sometimes absurd, and even repellant, and we are disgusted by Gulliver's exaggerated devotion to them.[7]

Particularly offputting is their absence of what would normally be called natural affection, for the Houyhnhnms love the species as a whole, rather than particular individuals, distinguishing only on the grounds of superior virtue. Thus 'they have no fondness [that is, foolish affection] for their colts and foals' (*GT* 316), and marriages are seen as purely practical arrangements. We are told 'courtship, love, presents, jointures, settlements, have no place in their thoughts, or terms whereby to express them in their language' (*GT* 317). The inclusion of 'love' in an enumeration of the financial aspects of matrimony satirises the mercenary marriages of eighteenth-century Britain, where love was often treated as an exchangeable commodity comparable with presents and settlements. But it also serves to undermine our image of Houyhnhnmland as the quintessentially happy polity.

This impression of unnaturalness is reinforced later in the voyage when we hear of the horse whose social call was delayed because her husband happened to drop dead that morning. Although somewhat inconvenienced by the need to find a suitable spot where his body could be placed, the widow 'behaved herself at our house as cheerfully as the rest' (*GT* 323). Although Swift sought to subdue his own personal feelings and griefs, and to cultivate stoicism, the extent of this equine equanimity seems far from desirable. In a famous letter to Pope, Swift argued against the concept of the human species as '*animal rationale*', suggesting instead that it was '*animal rationis capax*' (not a rational animal, but an animal capable of reason). The character of the Houyhnhnms exposes the extent of the disparity between mankind and a creature whose actions are shown to be entirely rational. If we were '*animal rationale*', we would behave like the Houyhnhnms, but the fact that we are not makes it difficult for us to sympathise with them. Indeed, it is difficult to believe that with all our irrational Yahoo passions, we are capable, as a species, of the kind of reason epitomised by the philosophic detachment of the Houyhnhnms. Nor may we be capable of recognising this reason as ideal or desirable.

The suspicion that the Houyhnhnms are rather unfeeling is compounded by the description of the general Assembly. The way that this is organised bears certain similarities to the conduct of the polity in Thomas More's *Utopia*. For one of the first tasks of the assembled Houyhnhnms is to:

Enquire into the state and condition of the several districts, whether they abound or be deficient in hay or oats or cows or Yahoos? And wherever there is any want (which is but seldom) it is immediately supplied by unanimous consent and contribution. (*GT* 318)

A comparable system of centralised planning operates in More's Utopia, for the prime function of the Utopian senate is to: 'Determine what commodity is in plenty in each particular place and again where on the island the crops have been meager. They at once fill up the scarcity of one place by the surplus of another.'[8] In practice, however, the Houyhnhnms are far less benign than this organisational function would suggest. They debate not the redistribution but the extermination of Yahoos, in order to work out the most rational course of action. Even the less severe recommendation that the Yahoos be merely castrated needs to be seen in the context of the Houyhnhnm master's earlier reaction to the 'savagery' of the European castration of horses (*GT* 288). The terms of the debate (which, incidentally appear to contradict Gulliver's earlier assertion that difference of opinion is unknown in Houyhnhnmland) may be taken as an indication that the dictates of reason are not invariably consonant with those other guides of human conduct, morality and humanity.

This brings in the second aspect of the critique of the Houyhnhnms, which is their inadequacy on the score of religion. A number of critics have argued that a devout Anglican like Swift could not have intended the atheistic Houyhnhnms to be seen as ideal. Some support for this argument might be drawn from Swift's religious writings, and in particular his sermons. In the sermon 'On the Testimony of Conscience', for instance, Swift argues 'that there is no solid, firm Foundation for Virtue, but on a Conscience which is guided by Religion'.[9] For 'if the Motives of our Actions be not resolved and determined into the Law of God, they will be precarious and uncertain, and liable to perpetual changes'.[10] Principles such as 'Moral Honesty', 'Honour', 'Reason' and 'Duty' are assessed for their efficacy in guiding conduct, and having been weighed in the balance are found wanting. Likewise in 'A Sermon upon the Excellency of Christianity' Swift questions the tendency of his contemporaries to admire the wisdom of the ancient philosophers, and exalt it over the writings of Christian thinkers. This preference for pagans is seen by Swift as an oblique attempt to traduce Christian revelation.[11]

Yet although this may seem to suggest that Swift could not have endorsed the society of the pagan Houyhnhnms, some caution is needed in reading across from one work of literature to another, and in particular from one form of writing to another. We have already seen that writers like Swift were perfectly prepared to write different things in different discourses or genres – in fact, the conventions and demands of the various forms made this a virtual necessity. It would hardly be surprising if Swift's sermons manifested a rather different perspective from a work of political satire/fiction like *Gulliver's Travels*. Indeed one such conflict is immediately evident – for while the sermonising Swift attacks the trend to celebrate ancient philosophers, Gulliver exalts just these characters in book three of his *Travels*. So the fact that reason without Christianity is not seen as an adequate code of behaviour in the sermons does not necessarily mean that the same will be true in the rather different world of the novel.

Even so, the absence of religion or even spirituality amongst the horses comes across as part of a general soullessness. The Houyhnhnms are free from the error and superstition that *A Tale of a Tub* identifies as characteristic of the history of the Christian churches since the early fathers. They do not have the great shoulder-knots of religious pageantry, but on the other hand they also lack the coats 'of very good cloth'[12] that represent Christian doctrine. This has led to suggestions that the Houyhnhnms embody either an irreligious or atheistic group within society, or an abstract capacity for reason in humankind. The former view, and in some ways also the latter view, is held by Irvin Ehrenpreis, who argues that:

The Houyhnhnms represent in general (though not wholly) what he considered to be a deistic view of human nature – a view against which, as a devout Anglican, he fought. By 'deistic' I mean the vague tradition in which men like Swift tended to lump freethinkers, deists, Socinians, and some latitudinarians.[13]

Moreover:

As admirable creatures, the Houyhnhnms represent what could be accomplished by beings . . . capable of pursuing the natural virtues summed up in reason and given us by nature at one remove from God; in their way – which is not the human way – they are perfect, and do not want religion. As absurd creatures, they represent the deistic presumption that mankind has no need of the specifically Christian virtues. Gulliver is misled as, in *Joseph Andrews*, Mr Wilson is ruined by a club of 'philosophers' who 'governed themselves by the infallible guide of human reason'.[14]

The horses embody the advantages but also the limitations of an adherence to reason, and therefore epitomise the deists, or Lockian philosophers, in the particular satire, while in the general satire they represent a human capacity for reason that is to be contrasted with the passion of the Yahoos.

There are elements of truth in both the soft and the hard readings, for Swift manifests an acute consciousness of the ambivalent position of the human individual, torn between reason and passion, the primitive and the civilised. Houyhnhnmland is therefore utopian or distopian, depending on which aspect of the reader's psyche is in the ascendant. At the same time, the satire operates on a social level, revealing a similar ambiguity. The Yahoos represent the lower and the Houyhnhnms the upper classes – the Yahoos the colonial oppressed and the Houyhnhnms the colonial oppressors. The narrative explores the negative and positive aspects of a civilised culture that is built on the maintenance of a savage and primitive underclass. But it also analyses the sensation of racial and cultural dispossession. Gulliver is caught between Yahoos and Houyhnhnms, just as Swift believed himself to be caught between the Irish and the English. The experience of alienation may be identified as having contributed to sending Gulliver mad, while the form of his madness constitutes the ultimate example of that human pretension to rationality which attempts to deny physical reality. Try as he might, Gulliver will never be a Houyhnhnm, and for him to pretend otherwise represents a failure to reconcile himself with the implications of his humanity. The need for such a reconciliation is emphasised throughout Swift's *oeuvre* through references to the bodily functions, which are seen to provide a continual reminder to the various human senses of the corporeal realities with which the human spirit is weighed down.

In his essay 'Ecriture and Eighteenth Century Fiction', Terry Eagleton brings out the structural significance of Gulliver's uncertain position:

> Gulliver despises men as Yahoos and identifies with the Houyhnhnms, the Houyhnhnms despise the Yahoos and regard Gulliver as one of them; we are amused by the Houyhnhnms and by Gulliver's delusions, but are close enough to the Yahoos for the amusement to be uneasy; and to cap it all there are some ways in which the Yahoos *are* superior to men. There is no way for the reader to 'totalise' these contradictions, which the text so adroitly springs upon him; he is merely caught in their dialectical interplay, rendered as eccentric to himself as the lunatic Gulliver, unable to turn to the refuge of an assuring authorial voice. To reconstruct the reader, reducing him from positioned subject to a function of polyphonic discourses: this is the *ideological* intervention accomplished by all Swift's writing.[15]

Both the way we evaluate the Yahoos and Houyhnhnms and the way we read the text are fundamentally influenced by Gulliver's behaviour on and after leaving the island. He tells us:

> As I was going to prostrate myself to kiss his hoof, he did me the honour to raise it gently to my mouth. I am not ignorant how much I have been censured for mentioning this last particular. For my detractors are pleased to think it improbable, that so illustrious a person should descend to give so great a mark of distinction to a creature so inferior as I. Neither have I forgot,

> how apt some travellers are to boast of extraordinary favours they have received. But if these censurers were better acquainted with the noble and courteous disposition of the Houyhnhnms, they would soon change their opinion. (*GT* 331)

Such excessive humility is reminiscent of the satire on the social system of Lilliput, and casts doubt on Gulliver's reliability as a witness or reporter. Any faith the reader may have had in the authorial judgement on Houyhnhnm society is progressively challenged, as the extent of Gulliver's delusions are made manifest.

In particular the repellant image of the Yahoos is in striking contrast to the behaviour of the Portuguese captain, Pedro de Mendez, who is a model of courtesy, honesty and generosity, and far more tolerant than most of us would be under similar circumstances. The narrative emphasises the contrast between on the one hand Gulliver's reception – the sailors are 'honest Portuguese'; they treat him 'with great humanity'; they give him 'chicken and some excellent wine' and 'a very clean cabin' – and on the other, Gulliver's 'silent and sullen' reaction (*GT* 335–6). The more we see Gulliver amongst his fellow humans, the more we are forced to recognise that contact with the horses has done little to improve his manners, and seems to have done much to touch his wits.

Thus Gulliver, his nose stopped with rue, is returned to his luckless and long-suffering family, where we leave him talking to his horses in the stable. This is not the end of the novel, however, for Gulliver appends a final chapter to the final voyage, which, at least to start with, is not so much the product of the whinnying idiot of chapter eleven, as a grand survey of the whole of the work, drawing out the political conclusions and reflecting on the nature of the travel-writing genre.

6

Nationalism/Colonialism: The Ambiguities of Ideology

In line with the ironic style of the *Travels*, the opening of Gulliver's final chapter is stuffed with spurious protestations that he has 'not been so studious of ornament as of truth'; that his 'principal design was to inform and not to amuse' (*GT* 340), with various aspersions cast in the direction of other travel writers, who, it is suggested, would do well to imitate the prosaic verity of our hero. This is all part of the general satire on the notorious fallacies of travellers' tales, but the repeated assertions that the writer's 'sole intention was the PUBLIC GOOD' (*GT* 341) need also to be read in the light of the prevalent eighteenth-century obsession with the moral function of literature. In the early years of the century even works of rather dubious moral value were often copiously larded with prefatory references to their improving qualities, and their importance as an antidote to the observable decline in the moral fibre of the young.

Appeals to the didactic significance of literature were something of a tradition, and in part derived from the need to justify the propagation of a popular, often profitable, but not very respectable form of writing. But this does not mean that they should be dismissed as insincere or 'mere convention'. The fact that writers found it necessary to make claims for the moral significance of their works is indicative of the strength of the beliefs firstly that fiction needed justification, and secondly that this could be found in the privileging of the didactic elements of the story. Later in the century, Samuel Johnson epitomised the moral view of the novel form in his assertion that:

> These books are written chiefly to the young, the ignorant and the idle, to whom they serve as lectures of conduct, and introductions into life. They are the entertainment of minds unfurnished with ideas, and therefore easily susceptible of impressions; not fixed by principles, and therefore easily following the current of fancy; not informed by experience, and consequently open to every false suggestion and partial account.

Defoe, Fielding and Richardson used the novel form to inculcate a code of virtue – Richardson through the creation of exemplary characters, Defoe and Fielding through a combination of authorial precepts and a portrayal of the moral value of experience. But the moral significance of Swift's work is rather less obvious. The claims for the virtuous tendency of the text come at the end of a narrative in which moral certainties have been very difficult to pin down.

Gulliver's narrative strategy does not provide a simple preceptual morality. There are no clearly and unequivocally exemplary characters, and no authoritative narrative voice to point up the moral of the story, and lay down the line on how the work should be interpreted. As we have seen over and over again in the reading of *Gulliver's Travels*, Swift's style serves not so much to 'inform' but to destabilise the readers, forcing them to question the nature of their society, but also the nature of their relationship with the text. There is a political message, but one which the readers must disentangle from the multifold ironies, and so experience not as subjects but as autonomous agents. Gulliver leaves 'the judicious reader to his own remarks and applications' (*GT* 341).

It is possible to read the political ideology of *Gulliver's Travels* not as a discreet entity, a 'content' to be separated from 'form', but as intimately connected with the narrative strategy. For Swift's opposition to the concentration of political power, with his emphasis on the need for a balanced constitution, and his fear of either dictatorship or oligarchy, is paralleled by his opposition to the concentration of narrative power. The flexible satiric structure that is the hallmark of *Gulliver's Travels*, with the resultant radical decentring of the subject, is a kind of narrative republicanism that dramatises the Tory republicanism of Swift's political perspective. As narrator Gulliver is like a constitutional ruler, whose powers are bounded by the consent of the readership, which may be withdrawn whenever he is perceived to have overstepped the mark. Moreover the topsy-turvy world of shifting perspectives is an appropriate medium in which to represent a political system which Swift sees as fundamentally corrupt and unbalanced – in which the limitations of the constitution are compounded by the corruption of the administration.

The fact that Swift provides a radical critique of the present system does not, however, mean, as Fabricant seems to suggest, that we should see his politics as progressive rather than conservative. The animus of Swift's attack on the injustices and inequalities of the present system was drawn not from a vision of the future, but from a profoundly influential rhetoric of how things were in the past. The republicanism that breathes through the narrative of *Gulliver's Travels* was in no way demotic, and should not be confused with the democratic ethos that emerged in the course of the nineteenth century. Swift's was an essentially Tory republicanism, that harked back to the administration of pre-Imperial Rome, and emphasised the role of public service, self-sacrifice and frugality in the administration of the country. For Swift the key to sound government lay not in empowering the suffering peasantry whom he saw to be oppressed by the present system, but rather in re-establishing the Ancient Constitution by ensuring that political influence, and with it a sense of social responsibility, was in the hands of those who owned the lands on which the peasants starved. The oligarchy of the Whigs was seen as a source of corruption that percolated through society as a whole. This kind of executive government should therefore be replaced by fully functioning houses of parliament, which could represent the interests of the country, and put a check on the power of the king. To get back to the analogy between Swift's text and his political ethos, the land-owning electorate would be, like the readers of *Gulliver's Travels*, autonomous agents.

Thus although the narrative of *Gulliver's Travels* appeals to the interpretative powers of the public, it is not directed to that general public which in the eighteenth century would have been described as 'the mob'. Swift's constituency is an enfranchised public, which may participate in the narrative polity because it has a knowledge of the events and people satirised in the text. The political allegory of *Gulliver's Travels* serves to denominate the work's public – it sorts out those who are qualified to evaluate the text from the disenfranchised mob who cannot, for both irony and satire operate by the presentation of a text that means one thing at face value, although we as sophisticated readers know that it really means quite another. Our pleasure in deciphering the text is in part derived from seeing ourselves as members of a reading elite, separated from a fictional class of credulous fools, who are incapable of true participation in the narrative.

I think it could be argued that many other 'readerly' texts also embody this kind of selection process, although often in a less obvious way. There may be no right or wrong reading, but the whole concept of narrative, with its appeals to previous knowledge, and subtleties of discrimination, suggests that there are right or at least wrong readers. Where the narrative is based on allegory, irony and satire, the implicit construction of readers as an elite measured against an ever present standard of misinterpretation is even more pronounced.

The generally favourable reception of *Gulliver's Travels* immediately following its publication indicates that Swift's political vision was not perceived as radically destabilising, but rather accorded with contemporary partisan rhetoric. It also suggests that the chaotic element in the satiric structure was accepted as part of the disorienting world of political allegory. As such, it can be seen as a sign of the looseness and flexibility of the fiction of the early eighteenth century, for the readers were prepared to be the victims of elaborate narrative games in a way that was not the case with later generations of consumers. At the more popular end of the market, Swift's readers had been brought up on fictions which frequently lacked the reassuring authoritative narrative placing that came to characterise the novel in the second half of the century. The higher-status readers came to *Gulliver's Travels* from traditions of political journalism or philosophical allegory, which constantly demanded the kind of active reading process that has been emphasised by modern critical theorists. A willingness to engage in a dialogue with the text was therefore combined with an openness resulting from a lack of readerly expectations.

What the high-status readers did object to was the particular satire, but also, as we have seen, the verisimilitude. This aspect of the work, that was to become almost the defining feature of the novel genre in the nineteenth century, was censured in the 1720s as 'low', and inappropriate for a serious work of moral and political fiction. In part this was due to the rather anal nature of Swift's conception of the 'everyday', but it also indicates that at the time of the publication of the *Travels*, there was no full recognition of the 'public' significance of the private and the ordinary. The explicit justifications of fiction tended to be located in its general moral or political significance. Truth was not seen as being 'truth to life', but truth to general universal principles or ideas. In the language of twentieth-century theory, the fiction was preoccupied with the *vrai* rather than *vraisemblance*.

In the course of the eighteenth century, however, the role of verisimilitude was increasingly accepted, and the novel began to be identified as a suitable form for the portrayal of 'ordinary experience'. Alongside this development, there was a growing tendency for novels to provide a more straightforward, ostensibly less demanding, role for the reader. As the novel became associated with the articulation of social morality, the readership became less accustomed to the kind of disorienting reading experience provided by *Gulliver's Travels*. As a result, misreadings began to emerge, as an audience schooled by a literature based on authorial authority sought to see Gulliver as an unimpeachable narrator, inculcating a moral ideal.

This model of *Gulliver's Travels* tended to reduce the political significance of the text to the presentation of a series of particular allegories – on Bolingbroke's escape to France, the signing of the Treaty of Utrecht, the debate between Protestants and Catholics and so on. For the emergence of the political themes depends to a large extent on the reader's participation in the narrative structure. It is only once we are distanced from Gulliver that we can identify the changing but recurrent rhetoric on the importance of a sound constitution and virtuous administration, or the personal and political corruption that are identified as a consequence of the spread of luxury and commercial expansion, but above all it is only when the reader takes an active role within the text that he or she is able to experience the nature of the narrative assault on colonialism. Once the ironic role of Gulliver is emphasised, it is clear that all the *Travels* serve, in rather different ways, to undermine the concept that European races are somehow more civilised than, and superior to, the natives of other countries. When seen in the context of his various host societies, Gulliver's nationalism and imperialistic prejudice are satirised as blindness, stupidity, or even evidence of evil. Perspective is used to ridicule the whole idea of colonial voyages of 'discovery'. From the point of view of the inhabitants, Gulliver's islands do not need to be 'found', because they were never 'lost'. The articulation of this idea within a travel narrative is rather ironic, for this form was often used to celebrate colonial expansion and new 'discoveries'.

The strength and significance of Gulliver's (Swift's?) sentiments on the subject of colonial conquest are finally brought home in a relatively unequivocal form, in the final chapter of the book:

> To say the truth, I had conceived a few scruples with relation to the distributive justice of princes upon those occasions. For instance, a crew of pirates are driven by a storm they know not whither, at length a boy discovers land from the topmast, they

go on shore to rob and plunder; they see an harmless people, are entertained with kindness, they give the country a new name, they take formal possession of it for the King, they set up a rotten plank or a stone for a memorial, they murder two or three dozen of the natives, bring away a couple more by force for a sample, return home, and get their pardon. Here commences a new dominion acquired with a title by *divine right*. Ships are sent with the first opportunity, the natives driven out or destroyed, their princes tortured to discover their gold; a free licence given to all acts of inhumanity and lust, the earth reeking with the blood of its inhabitants: and this execrable crew of butchers employed in so pious an expedition, is a *modern colony* sent to convert and civilize an idolatrous and barbarous people. (*GT* 343–4)

The applicability of this to British imperial expansion is underscored by the irony of Gulliver's disclaimer that:

This description, I confess, doth by no means affect the British nation, who *may* be an example to the whole world for their wisdom, care and justice in planting colonies; their liberal endowments for the advancement of religion and learning; their choice of devout and able pastors to propagate Christianity; their caution in stocking their provinces with people of sober lives and conversations from this the mother kingdom; their strict regard to the distribution of justice, in supplying the civil administration through all their Colonies with officers of the greatest abilities, utter strangers to corruption; and to crown all, by sending the most vigilant and virtuous Governors, who have no other views than the happiness of the people over whom they preside, and the honour of the King their master. (my italics) (*GT* 344)

The reader well knows how to read that 'may', for British colonial administration was a by-word for corruption and inefficiency, making the domestic system look like a model of public virtue by comparison.

This attack on colonialism was not tangential but integral to the Tory rhetoric, for the growth of colonial trade was seen as part and parcel of the commercial expansion that was leading to the perversion of the natural processes of production and consumption that represented the domestic economy of the country. Foreign trade and foreign goods were almost synonymous with luxury and corruption to the die-hard Tory thinkers of the seventeenth and early eighteenth century, for they necessitated the complex financial systems that were seen to be sapping the nation, distracting attention from the cultivation of agriculture and industry.

But to Swift colonial expansion also had moral connota-tions, as a result of his experiences in Ireland. Swift had seen at first hand how an occupying power could cripple the economy and sap the very vitals of a nation. Yet the ambivalent status of Ireland, as at once a foreign country and part of the mother-land, made it possible for Swift to elide and cut with facility between the analysis of colonial dominance and an analysis of class. The relationship between the absentee landlords of Ireland and their starving peasant tenants was one of colonial master to native, but also of social elite to underclass. The subjugation of Ireland by England may be dramatised in the Lindalinian rebellion, but in addition both book three and book four represent an analysis of the social and psychological implications of dominance in general. They provide an investi-gation of the social consequences of those more abstract ideas about the political system which are explored in books one and two.

Yet while much of the *Travels* can be read as an articulate attack on the system of colonialism, the narrative is character-istically equivocal in relation to the concept of the primitive. The voice of Swift the Irish patriot is balanced by the voice of Swift the actor on the English political stage – the desperate seeker for a living within England. For while Gulliver con-demns the brutality of imperialism, and there is a level at which the narrative celebrates the absence of pretension amongst the Yahoos, there is an instinctive repugnance towards those ideas of physicality and lack of restraint which are associated with primitivism and which echo conventional eighteenth-century ideas of the nature of the masses and the 'mob'. But the real horror within Swift's narrative is the idea that when it comes to the crunch we are all essentially primitive. The revelation of the true nature of the human species, and of the dangerous sexuality that underlies female playfulness, provides a gloss to the political text – a warning that any political system will have to be able to restrain such potentially destabilising private impulses.

The perception of the primitive beneath the veneer of civilisation does not ultimately serve, however, to undermine the country party perspective. Despite Swift's suspicions, it is still to the landed classes that he looks for a measure of stability that cannot be attained by the landless masses. The excremental vision that recurs throughout *Gulliver's Travels* is thus not taken to its logical political conclusion, for that conclusion would involve an adherence to democracy that would be utterly anachronistic. Instead Swift harks back to the yeomen of Old England, and his suggestion in book three that these have declined in size over the centuries takes us back to the enormous farmers of Brobdingnag, suggesting that size may on occasions be equated with moral worth.

The voyages to Lilliput and Brobdingnag enforce the importance of a virtuous administration, which in Brobdingnag is shown to be based on an integrated but hierarchical system, and a concern for the domestic to the exclusion of all supranational commercial or foreign policy considerations. As a result, Brobdingnag is identified as the least corrupt of the Yahoo nations, and its 'wise maxims in morality and government it would be our happiness to observe' (*GT* 341). In other words, we should abandon expansionist, imperialistic, colonial policies, and concentrate on the development of a face-to-face society, based not on the oppression of one distant class by another, but on the total integration of the community in a carefully graduated hierarchy in which everyone knows their place and cooperates for the good of the whole.

In many ways, *Gulliver's Travels* can be seen as a moral and improving text, even though it does not conform to the conventional models of fictional didacticism. It ends, after all, with an exhortation against the moral vice of pride. Yet this elision of the moral and political themes ensures that the autonomy even of the elite reader, and the model of narrative republicanism, are to some extent more apparent than real. As we have seen in analysing critical reactions to the *Travels*, opinions have differed widely over how to interpret the tale, and the flexible role of Gulliver as alternately reliable narrator and gullible fool emphasises the need for an active approach to the text. But however loose and evasive it may appear, the narrative does impose parameters on interpretation, and in many ways these are the more pervasive for being hard to pin down. We are not told what to think, although the absence of definitive authorial statements may not be entirely liberating, but rather encourage us to believe that what we are *led* to think represents opinions that we have reached ourselves. We experience the moral consequences of colonialism or political corruption, we witness the foolish blindness of nationalistic prejudice, and that is all very well. But in identifying the Tory rhetoric as a moral rather than a political or factional perspective, we might be seen to be falling into the narrative trap, by swallowing prejudices as universal truths.

The text of *Gulliver's Travels* operates by a subtle combination of readerly autonomy and political propaganda. The public are invited to participate in the commonwealth of interpretation, but in the fictional as in the political sphere, that participation is to a large extent controlled by pre-existent rhetorical paradigms. We have to fall in with the consensus to some extent, and even what we believe to be our own opinions are greatly influenced by the opinions of others, and above all by the nature of the ideological choices presented to us. So while the recent critical theorists have done a signal service to literary criticism in emphasising the importance of readerly choice and participation, we also need to recognise the elements of benevolent dictatorship lurking within the narrative polity of early eighteenth-century fiction at least.

Notes

HISTORICAL AND CULTURAL CONTEXT

1. See Clark, *English Society*.
2. Downie, *Jonathan Swift*, pp. 135–63.
3. Traugott, 'A Tale of a Tub', p. 84.
4. Sir Thomas More, *Utopia*, vol IV of *Complete Works* ed. Edward Surtz and J. H. Hexter (New Haven, Yale University Press, 1965); Erasmus, *Encomium Moriae* (1515) translated as *In Praise of Folly* by Betty Radice, introduction and notes by A. H. T. Levi (Harmondsworth, Penguin, 1971).
5. François Rabelais, *The Histories of Gargantua and Pantagruel*, translated J. M. Cohen (Harmondsworth, Penguin, 1955).
6. Downie, *Jonathan Swift*, p. 267.
7. Fabricant, *Swift's Landscape*, pp. 19–21.
8. Sir William Temple, *Essay upon the Advancement of Trade in Ireland* in *Miscellanea*, 2nd ed. (London, 1681), p. 111.
9. Swift, *Drapier's Letters*, *Prose Works* X, p. 103.
10. On the rise of the novel see Davis, *Factual Fictions*, and McKeon, *Origins*.

CRITICAL RECEPTION

1. *Correspondence* III, 180.
2. *Correspondence* III, 181.
3. *Correspondence* III, 182.
4. *Correspondence* III, 181.
5. *Correspondence* III, 182–3.
6. *Correspondence* III, 179.

7. Published in Abel Boyer's *The Political State of Great Britain* (Nov. 1726 – Jan. 1727, XXXII, pp. 460–99; 515–45; XXXIII, 1–27) XXXIII, 27.
8. Swift, *Prose Works of Jonathan Swift D.D.*, ed. Temple Scott (London, 1899) IX, p. 110.
9. Downie, 'Political Characterization' and *Jonathan Swift*; F. P. Lock, *The Politics of Gulliver's Travels*.
10. Samuel Johnson, *Lives of the English Poets* (London, Everyman's Library, 1925, 1961) II, 261.
11. Kathleen Williams (ed), *Swift: The critical heritage*, p. 67.
12. Beattie, 'On Fable and Romance', in *Dissertations Moral and Critical* (Dublin, 1783) I, 245–7.
13. T. B. Macaulay, *Works*, Albany edition (London, 1908) VIII, 307.
14. Thackeray, 'Swift', in *The English Humourists of the Eighteenth Century* (London, 1853) Grey Walls Press ed. (London, 1949), p. 33.
15. Leslie Stephen, *Jonathan Swift* (1882) (London, Macmillan, 1931), p. 183.
16. Nicolson and Mohler, 'Scientific Background'.
17. George Orwell, 'Politics vs. Literature: An examination of *Gulliver's Travels*', in *Shooting an Elephant and other Essays* (1950), reprinted *Fair Liberty* ed. A. Norman Jeffares, pp. 166–85.
18. Brown, 'Excremental Vision', p. 95.
19. *ibid.*, p. 96.
20. *ibid.*, p. 101.
21. Traugott, 'The Yahoo', p. 136.
22. Orwell, 'Politics vs. Literature', p. 179.

THEORETICAL PERSPECTIVES

1. Wolfgang Iser, *The Act of Reading* (London, Routledge and Kegan Paul, 1978).
2. Roland Barthes, 'The Death of the Author', in *The Rustle of Language*, translated Richard Howard (Oxford, Blackwell, 1986), pp. 49–50.
3. Michel Foucault, 'What is an Author?', in *Textual Strategies: Perspectives in post–structuralist criticism*, ed. Josue V. Harari (Ithaca, Cornell University Press, 1979), p. 143.
4. Michel Foucault, *The Archaeology of Knowledge*, translated A. M. Sheridan Smith (London, Tavistock, 1972).
5. For a definitive account of Russian formalism see Viktor Erlich, *Russian Formalism: History-doctrine* (The Hague, Mouton, 1955; revised ed. 1965).

6. Roland Barthes, *S/Z*, translated Richard Miller (London, Cape, 1975).
7. Viktor Shklovsky, 'Sterne's *Tristram Shandy*', in Lee T. Lemon and Marion J. Reiss, eds and trans, *Russian Formalist Criticism: Four essays* (Lincoln, University of Nebraska Press, 1965), pp. 25–57, p. 57.

1. FACT/FICTION: SOME AMBIGUITIES

1. See Percy G. Adams, *Travelers and Travel Liars, 1660–1800* (Berkeley, University of California Press, 1962); Arthur Sherbo, 'Swift and Travel Literature', *Modern Language Studies* 9, no. 3 (1979); Philip. B. Gove, *The Imaginary Voyage*.
2. William Dampier, *A New Voyage Round the World* (1697) with an introduction by Sir Albert Gray (London, Adam and Charles Black, 1937). Also Willard H. Bonner, *Captain William Dampier: Buccaneer-author* (Oxford, Oxford University Press, 1934).
3. *Correspondence* II, 431, 430.
4. Voight, *Swift and the Twentieth Century*, p. 72.
5. George Psalmanazar, *An Historical and Geographical Description of Formosa, an Island subject to the Emperor of Japan* (1704) reprinted in The Library of Impostors, London, undated, introduction.
6. Francis Bacon, *New Atlantis* (1627) in *Works*, ed. James Spedding, R. L. Ellis and D. N. Heath (London, 1857–74).
7. See Davis, *Factual Fictions*.
8. Henry MacKenzie, *The Man of Feeling* (1771), ed. Brian Vickers (Oxford, Oxford University Press, 1967).
9. Landa, *Swift and the Church of Ireland*, pp. 10–18.
10. Brown, 'Excremental Vision', p. 95.

2. LOOKING DOWN: LILLIPUT

1. See John Barrell, *English Literature in History, 1730–80* (London, Hutchinson Academic Press, 1983), pp. 31–50.
2. Compare the background of the narrative persona presented in the first issue of Joseph Addison's *Spectator*, 1 March, 1711.
3. Traugott, 'The Yahoo', p. 129.
4. See Pocock, *The Machiavellian Moment*, p. 427.
5. *ibid., passim*.

6. Rogers, *Eighteenth-Century Encounters*, p. 7.
7. Traugott, 'The Yahoo', p. 130.
8. Lock, *Politics of Gulliver's Travels*, p. 68.
9. *ibid.*, p. 69.
10. e.g. Case, *Four Essays*, pp. 72–3; cf. Downie, *Jonathan Swift*, p. 276.
11. Lock, *Politics of Gulliver's Travels*, p. 35.
12. Case, *Four Essays*, pp. 74–5; Reilly, *Jonathan Swift*, pp. 180–1.
13. Case, *Four Essays*, p. 76.
14. Ehrenpreis, *Swift* II, 5–12; II, 622–34.
15. François Rabelais, *The Histories of Gargantua and Pantagruel*, translated J. M. Cohen (Harmondsworth, Penguin, 1955), p. 74.

3. LOOKING UP: BROBDINGNAG

1. Aldous Huxley, *Do What You Will* (1929) quoted in Brown, 'Excremental Vision', p. 92.
2. Fabricant, *Swift's Landscape*, p. 24.
3. Abel Boyer, 'Account and Abstract', in *The Political State of Great Britain* XXXIII, 27.
4. Henry St John, Viscount Bolingbroke, *Dissertation upon Parties*, (1734), 7th ed. (London, 1749), pp. 304–5.
5. For a full account of the debates over the standing army and the financial system in the early eighteenth century see Pocock, *The Machiavellian Moment*, pp. 423–62.

4. FLYING AROUND: LAPUTA

1. Nicolson and Mohler, 'Scientific Background', p. 228.
2. Rogers, *Eighteenth-Century Encounters*, p. 12.
3. Nicolson and Mohler, 'Scientific Background', pp. 233–4.
4. cf. chapter 13 of the *Memoirs of Martinus Scriblerus*, in *The Works of Alexander Pope*, vol. VI (London, 1760).
5. Fabricant, *Swift's Landscape*, p. 160.
6. Nicolson and Mohler, 'Scientific Background', pp. 240–8.
7. For an authoritative account of scientific developments in the early eighteenth century see Hunter, *Science and Society*.
8. Ferguson, *Swift and Ireland*, pp. 86–7.

9. William Coxe, *Memoirs of the Life and Administration of Sir Robert Walpole, Earl of Orford*, 3 vols (London, T. Cadell, Jun. & W. Davies, 1798), I, 217.
10. Swift, *Drapier's Letters*, *Prose Works* X, p. 7.
11. Lock, *Politics of Gulliver's Travels*, p. 85.
12. Case, *Four Essays*, pp. 81–2.
13. Rogers, *Eighteenth-Century Encounters*, pp. 18–19.
14. Jacob, *Newtonians*, p. 54.
15. G. Ravenscroft Dennis, (ed.) *Gulliver's Travels*, volume VIII of *Prose Works of Jonathan Swift D.D.*, ed. Temple Scott, p. 181n; Philip Griffith, 'Swift's Munodi and Bolingbroke, a Firmer Identification', *South Central Bulletin*, no. 36 (Winter, 1976), 145–6.
16. Sir Charles Firth, 'The Political Significance of *Gulliver's Travels*', p 230; Downie, 'Political Characterization', pp. 116–17.
17. Case, *Four Essays*, p. 87.
18. Abel Boyer, *The Political State of Great Britain* XXXII, 525–6.
19. Francis Bacon, *Works*, ed. James Spedding, R. L. Ellis and D. N. Heath (London, 1857–74) II, 156.
20. English translation of Newton's *Principia* by Florian Cajoli (Berkeley, University of California Press, 1934) Cotes' preface, pp. xx–xxi.
21. Sprat, *History*, part two, quoted in Probyn, *Jonathan Swift*, p. 59.
22. Hunter, *Science and Society*, p. 16.

5. OUT TO GRASS: HOUYHNHNMLAND

1. Swift, *Tale of a Tub*, *Prose Works* I, p. 49.
2. Brown, 'Excremental Vision', p. 96.
3. Fabricant, *Swift's Landscape*, p. 35.
4. *ibid.*
5. McKeon, *Origins*, p. 350.
6. McKeon, *Origins*, p. 351.
7. Kathleen Williams, 'Gulliver's Voyage to the Houyhnhnms', p. 258.
8. Sir Thomas More, *Complete Works*, ed. Edward Surtz and J. H. Hexter (New Haven, Yale University Press, 1965) IV, 147.
9. Swift, *Works* IX, 152.
10. *ibid.* IX, 154.
11. *ibid.* IX, 242.
12. Swift, *Tale*, *Prose Works* I, p. 49.
13. Ehrenpreis, 'The Origins of *Gulliver's Travels*', in *Fair Liberty*, ed. Norman Jeffares, p. 212.
14. *ibid.*, p. 214.
15. Eagleton, 'Ecriture', in *Literature, Society*, p. 58.

Select Bibliography

WORKS BY SWIFT

The Correspondence of Jonathan Swift, ed. Harold Williams, 5 vols (Oxford, Oxford University Press, 1965).
Jonathan Swift: The complete poems, ed. Pat Rogers (Harmondsworth, Penguin, 1983).
The Prose Works of Jonathan Swift, ed. Herbert Davis, 14 vols (Oxford, Blackwell, 1939–68).

CRITICAL WORKS

Bony, Alain, 'Call Me Gulliver', *Poetique* 14 (1973) 197–209.
Boyer, Abel, 'Account and Abstract of *GT*', in *The Political State of Great Britain* (Nov. 1726 – Jan. 1727, XXXII, pp. 460–99; 515–45; XXXIII, 1–27).
Brown, Norman O., 'The Excremental Vision', in *Discussions of Jonathan Swift*, ed. John Traugott, 92–104.
Carnochan, W.B., *Lemuel Gulliver's Mirror for Man* (Berkeley, CA, University of California Press, 1968).
Case, Arthur E., *Four Essays on 'Gulliver's Travels'* (Princeton, NJ, Princeton University Press, 1945) reprinted (Gloucester, Mass., Peter Smith, 1958).
Castle, Terry, 'Why the Houyhnhnms Don't Write: Swift, satire and the fear of the text', *Essays in Literature* 7 (1980) 31–44.
Clark, J. C. D., *English Society 1688–1832: Ideology, social structure and political practice during the ancien régime* (Cambridge, Cambridge University Press, 1985).

Select Bibliography

Clark, Paul Odell, 'A Gulliver Dictionary', *Studies in Philology*, L (1953) 592–624.

Clifford, James L., 'Gulliver's Fourth Voyage', in *Quick Springs of Sense: Studies in the eighteenth century*, ed. Larry S. Champion (Athens, GA, University of Georgia Press, 1974).

Cook, R. I., *Jonathan Swift as a Tory Pamphleteer* (Seattle, WA, Washington University Press, 1967).

Crane, R. S., 'The Houyhnhnms, the Yahoos and the History of Ideas', in J. A. Mazzeo, *Reason and the Imagination* (New York & London, Columbia University Press, 1962).

Davis, Lennard J., *Factual Fictions: The origins of the English novel* (New York, Columbia University Press, 1983).

Donoghue, Denis, *Jonathan Swift: A critical introduction* (Cambridge, Cambridge University Press, 1971).

Downie, John, 'Political Characterization in *Gulliver's Travels*', *Yearbook of English Studies* 7 (1977) 108–21.

Downie, John, *Jonathan Swift: Political writer* (Routledge, 1984).

Eagleton, Terry, 'Ecriture and Eighteenth Century Fiction', in *Literature, Society and the Sociology of Literature*, Proceedings of the conference held at the University of Essex, July, 1976 (University of Essex, 1977) 55–8.

Eddy, William, *Gulliver's Travels: A Critical Study* (Princeton, NJ, Princeton University Press, 1923).

Ehrenpreis, Irvin, *Swift: The man, his works and the age* (London, Methuen, 1962–83).

Elder, Lucius W., 'The Pride of the Yahoo', *Modern Language Notes* 35 (April, 1920) 206–11.

Ewald, W. B. Jnr, *The Masks of Jonathan Swift* (Cambridge, MA, Harvard University Press, 1954).

Fabricant, Carole, *Swift's Landscape* (Baltimore, MD, Johns Hopkins University Press, 1982).

Ferguson, Oliver W., *Jonathan Swift and Ireland* (Champaign, IL, University of Illinois Press, 1962).

Fink, Z. S., 'Political Theory in *Gulliver's Travels*', *Journal of English Literary History*, 14 (1947) 151–61.

Firth, Sir Charles, 'The Political Significance of *Gulliver's Travels*', *Proceedings of the British Academy* IX (1919–20) 237–50, reprinted in Sir Charles Firth, *Essays Historical and Literary* (Oxford, Clarendon Press, 1938).

Fussell, Paul, *The Rhetorical World of Augustan Humanism: Ethics and imagery from Swift to Burke* (Oxford, Clarendon Press, 1965).

Goldgar, Bertrand A., *Walpole and the Wits: The relation of politics to literature 1722–1742* (Lincoln, NB and London, University of Nebraska Press, 1976).

Select Bibliography

Gove, Philip B., *The Imaginary Voyage in Prose Fiction: A history of its criticism and a guide for its study, with an annotated check list of 215 imaginary voyages from 1700 to 1800* (New York, Columbia University Press, 1941).

Greenacre, Phyllis, *Swift and Carroll: A psychoanalytical study of two lives*, (New York, International Universities Press, 1955).

Greene, D. J., 'Recent Studies in the Restoration and Eighteenth Century', *Studies in English Literature*, I (1961), 115–41.

Guskin, Phyllis J., 'A Very Remarkable Book: Abel Boyer's view of *Gulliver's Travels*', *Studies in Philology* 72, (1975) 439–53.

Hammond, Brean, *Gulliver's Travels* (Milton Keynes, Open University Press, 1988).

Hardy, Evelyn, *The Conjured Spirit – Swift* (London, Hogarth Press, 1949).

Holly, Grant, 'Travel and Translation: Textuality in *Gulliver's Travels*', *Criticism* 21 (1979) 134–52.

Hunter, Michael, *Science and Society in Restoration England* (Cambridge, Cambridge University Press, 1981).

Jacob, Margaret, *The Newtonians and the English Revolution, 1689–1720* (Hemel Hempstead, Harvester Wheatsheaf, 1976).

Jeffares, A. Norman (ed.), *Fair Liberty Was All His Cry: A tercentenary tribute to Jonathan Swift 1667–1745* (London, Macmillan, 1967).

Jeffares, A. Norman (ed.), *Swift: Modern judgements* (London, Macmillan, 1968).

Jones, Myrddin, 'Swift, Harrington, and Corruption in England', *Philological Quarterly* 53 (1974) 59–70.

Kelling, Harold, 'Some Significant Names in *Gulliver's Travels*', *Studies in Philology* 48, no. 4 (October 1951).

Kramnick, Isaac, *Bolingbroke and his Circle: The politics of nostalgia in the age of Walpole* (Cambridge, MA, Harvard University Press, 1968).

Landa, Louis A., *Swift and the Church of Ireland* (Oxford, Clarendon Press, 1954).

Leavis, F. R., 'The Irony of Swift', *Scrutiny* 2 (March, 1934) 364–78, reprinted in F. R. Leavis, *Determinations* (London, Chatto and Windus, 1934) 79–108, and *The Common Pursuit* (London, Chatto and Windus, 1952).

Levine, Joseph M., *Dr Woodward's Shield: History, science and satire in Augustan England* (Berkeley, CA, University of California Press, 1977).

Lock, F. P., *The Politics of Gulliver's Travels* (Oxford, Oxford University Press, 1980).

McKeon, Michael, *The Origins of the English Novel* (Baltimore, MD, Johns Hopkins University Press, 1987; London, Radius, 1988).

Select Bibliography

Monk, Samuel H., 'The Pride of Lemuel Gulliver', *Sewanee Review* 63 (1955).

Nicolson, Marjorie and Mohler, Nora M., 'The Scientific Background of Swift's "Voyage to Laputa"', *Annals of Science* II (1937), reprinted in *Fair Liberty*, ed. Norman Jeffares, 226–69.

Nokes, David, *Jonathan Swift: A hypocrite reversed* (Oxford, Oxford University Press, 1985).

Nokes, David, *Raillery and Rage: A study of eighteenth-century satire* (Hemel Hempstead, Harvester Wheatsheaf, 1987).

Pocock, J. G. A., *The Machiavellian Moment: Florentine political thought and the Atlantic republican tradition* (Princeton, NJ, Princeton University Press, 1975).

Pollak, Ellen, *The Poetics of Sexual Myth: Gender and ideology in the verse of Swift and Pope* (Chicago, University of Chicago Press, 1985).

Probyn, Clive T. (ed.), *Jonathan Swift: The contemporary background* (Manchester, Manchester University Press, 1978).

Quintana, Ricardo, *The Mind and Art of Jonathan Swift* (Oxford, Oxford University Press, 1936; London, Methuen, 1953).

Quintana, Ricardo, 'Situational Satire: A commentary on the method of Swift', *University of Toronto Quarterly* XVII (1948) 130–6, reprinted in *Studies in the Literature of the Augustan Age: Essays in honor of A. E. Case*, ed. R. C. Boys (Ann Arbor, MI, George Wahr Publishing Co. for the Augustan Reprint Society 1952), 259–65.

Quintana, Ricardo, *Swift: An introduction* (Oxford, Oxford University Press, 1955).

Quintana, Ricardo, '*Gulliver's Travels*: Some structural properties and certain questions of critical approach and interpretation', in *The Character of Swift's Satire*, ed. Claude Rawson, 282–304.

Rawson, Claude J., *Gulliver and the Gentle Reader: Studies in Swift and our time* (London, Routledge, 1973).

Rawson, Claude, ed., *The Character of Swift's Satire: A revised focus* (London and Toronto, Associated University Presses, 1983).

Rawson, Claude and Mezciems, Jenny (eds), *English Satire and the Satiric Tradition* (Oxford, Basil Blackwell, 1984).

Reilly, Patrick, *Jonathan Swift: The brave desponder* (Manchester, Manchester University Press, 1982).

Robbins, Caroline, *The Eighteenth-Century Commonwealthman* (Cambridge, MA, Harvard University Press, 1961).

Rogers, Pat, *Eighteenth-Century Encounters: Studies in literature and society in the age of Walpole* (Hemel Hempstead, Harvester Wheatsheaf, 1985).

Rosenheim, Edward J. Jnr, *Swift and the Satirist's Art* (Chicago, University of Chicago Press, 1963).

Sherburn, George, 'Errors Concerning the Houyhnhnms', *Modern Philology* 56 (1958).

Smith, Roland M., 'Swift's Little Language and Nonsense Names', *Journal of English and Germanic Philology* LIII (1954) 178–96.

Sprat, Thomas, *The History of the Royal Society of London* (London, 1667) ed. J. I. Cape and H. W. Jones (London, Routledge, 1959).

Traugott, John (ed), *Discussions of Jonathan Swift* (Boston, MA, D. C. Heath & Co., 1962).

Traugott, John, 'A Tale of a Tub' in *The Character of Swift's Satire*, ed. Claude Rawson, 83–126.

Traugott, John, 'The Yahoo in the Doll's House: *Gulliver's Travels* the children's classic', in *English Satire and the Satiric Tradition*, ed. Claude Rawson and Jenny Mezciems, 127–50.

Tuveson, Ernest, 'Swift: The Dean as satirist', *University of Toronto Quarterly* (1953) 368–75.

Voight, Milton, *Swift and the Twentieth Century* (Detroit, MI, Wayne State University Press, 1964).

Welcher, Jeanne K. and Bush, George E. Jnr (eds), *Gulliveriana VI: Critiques of Gulliver's Travels and allusions thereto*, facsimile reprints (New York, Delmar, 1976).

Willey, Basil, 'A Note on Swift', *The Eighteenth-Century Background* (London, c. 1940; Chatto and Windus, 1980).

Williams, Harold, *Dean Swift's Library* (Cambridge, Cambridge University Press, 1932).

Williams, Kathleen, 'Gulliver's Voyage to the Houyhnhnms', *ELH, A Journal of English Literary History* XXI (1954) 193–207, reprinted in *Swift: Modern judgements*, ed. Norman Jeffares, 247–57.

Williams, Kathleen, *Jonathan Swift and the Age of Compromise* (Lawrence, KA & London, University of Kansas Press, 1958).

Williams, Kathleen (ed.), *Swift: The critical heritage* (London, Routledge, 1970).

Wood, Nigel, *Swift* (Hemel Hempstead, Harvester Wheatsheaf, 1986).

Zimmerman, Everett, *Swift's Narrative Strategies* (Ithaca, NY, Cornell University Press, 1983).

Index

Index

Index